I'll Be Your Plaything

33 1/3 Global

33 1/3 Global, a series related to but independent from **33 1/3**, takes the format of the original series of short, music-based books, and brings the focus to music throughout the world. With initial volumes focusing on Japanese and Brazilian music, the series will also include volumes on the popular music of Australia/Oceania, Europe, Africa, the Middle East, and more.

33 1/3 Japan

Series editor: Noriko Manabe

Spanning a range of artists and genres—from the 1970s rock of Happy End to technopop band Yellow Magic Orchestra, the Shibuya-kei of Cornelius, classic anime series *Cowboy Bebop,* J-Pop/EDM hybrid Perfume, and vocaloid star Hatsune Miku—33 1/3 Japan is a series devoted to in-depth examination of Japanese popular music of the twentieth and twenty-first centuries.

Published titles:

Supercell's *Supercell* by Keisuke Yamada

Yoko Kanno's *Cowboy Bebop Soundtrack* by Rose Bridges

Perfume's *Game* by Patrick St. Michel

Cornelius's *Fantasma* by Martin Roberts

Joe Hisaishi's *My Neighbor Totoro: Soundtrack* by Kunio Hara

Shonen Knife's *Happy Hour* by Brooke McCorkle

Nenes' *Koza Dabasa* by Henry Johnson

Forthcoming titles:

Yuming's *The 4th Moon* by Lasse Lehtonen

Yellow Magic Orchestra's *Yellow Magic Orchestra* by Toshiyuki Ohwada

Kohaku Uta Gassen: The Red and White Song Contest by Shelley Brunt

33 1/3 Brazil

Series editor: Jason Stanyek

Covering the genres of samba, tropicália, rock, hip hop, forró, bossa nova, heavy metal, and funk, among others, 33 1/3 Brazil is a series devoted to in-depth examination of the most important Brazilian albums of the twentieth and twenty-first centuries.

Published titles:

Caetano Veloso's *A Foreign Sound* by Barbara Browning

Tim Maia's *Tim Maia Racional Vols. 1 &2* by Allen Thayer

João Gilberto and Stan Getz's *Getz/Gilberto* by Brian McCann

Gilberto Gil's *Refazenda* by Marc A. Hertzman

Dona Ivone Lara's *Sorriso Negro* by Mila Burns

Milton Nascimento and Lô Borges's *The Corner Club* by Jonathon Grasse

Racionais MCs' *Sobrevivendo no Inferno* by Derek Pardue

Naná Vasconcelos's *Saudades* by Daniel B. Sharp

Forthcoming titles:

Jorge Ben Jor's *África Brasil* by Frederick J. Moehn

Chico Buarque's *Chico Buarque* by Charles A. Perrone

33 1/3 Europe

Series editor: Fabian Holt

Spanning a range of artists and genres, 33 1/3 Europe offers engaging accounts of popular and culturally significant albums of Continental Europe and the North Atlantic from the twentieth and twenty-first centuries.

Published titles:

Darkthrone's *A Blaze in the Northern Sky* by Ross Hagen

Ivo Papazov's *Balkanology* by Carol Silverman

Heiner Müller and Heiner Goebbels's *Wolokolamsker Chaussee* by
   Philip V. Bohlman

Modeselektor's *Happy Birthday!* by Sean Nye

Mercyful Fate's *Don't Break the Oath* by Henrik Marstal

I'll Be Your Plaything

Anna Szemere and András Rónai

Series editor: Fabian Holt

BLOOMSBURY ACADEMIC
NEW YORK • LONDON • OXFORD • NEW DELHI • SYDNEY

BLOOMSBURY ACADEMIC
Bloomsbury Publishing Inc
1385 Broadway, New York, NY 10018, USA
50 Bedford Square, London, WC1B 3DP, UK
29 Earlsfort Terrace, Dublin 2, Ireland

BLOOMSBURY, BLOOMSBURY ACADEMIC, and the Diana logo are
trademarks of Bloomsbury Publishing Plc

Library of Congress Cataloging-in-Publication Data

Names: Szemere, Anna, author. | Rónai, András, author.
Title: I'll be your plaything / Anna Szemere and András Rónai.
Description: New York : Bloomsbury Academic, 2022. |
Series: 33 1/3 Europe | Includes bibliographical references and index. |
Summary: "An overview of the 2010 concept album that drastically
re-imagines cover versions of Hungary's most popular hits from the
socialist era"– Provided by publisher.
Identifiers: LCCN 2021039985 (print) | LCCN 2021039986 (ebook) |
ISBN 9781501354434 (hardback) | ISBN 9781501354427 (paperback) |
ISBN 9781501354458 (pdf) | ISBN 9781501354441 (epub)
Subjects: LCSH: Palya, Bea, 1976–Criticism and interpretation. |
Palya, Bea, 1976-. Én leszek a játékszered. | Popular music–Hungary–
History and criticism. | Cover versions–Hungary–History and criticism. |
Communism and music–Hungary.
Classification: LCC ML420.P199 S94 2022 (print) |
LCC ML420.P199 (ebook) | DDC 781.6409439—dc23
LC record available at https://lccn.loc.gov/2021039985
LC ebook record available at https://lccn.loc.gov/2021039986

ISBN: HB: 978-1-5013-5443-4
       PB: 978-1-5013-5442-7
       ePDF: 978-1-5013-5445-8
       eBook: 978-1-5013-5444-1
       XML: 978-1-5013-5446-5

Typeset by RefineCatch Limited, Bungay, Suffolk
Printed and bound in the United States of America

Series: 33 1/3 Europe

To find out more about our authors and books visit www.bloomsbury.com
and sign up for our newsletters.

Contents

Figures

Acknowledgments

A number of our colleagues, friends, and family members encouraged, supported, and offered their valuable insight during the research and writing of this book. An enormous thank you goes to Bea Palya and Samu Gryllus for generously and enthusiastically sharing their time, attention, ideas, and memories with us regarding so many aspects of producing the album *Én leszek a játékszered* or, as they nicknamed it, ÉLJ. Without the vision, inspiring, and kind guidance of our series editor, Fabian Holt, this project would not have come to fruition. Leah Babb-Rosenfeld and the staff at Bloomsbury were patient and caring collaborators. We greatly benefited from the suggestions of the anonymous reviewers of our book proposal as well. Chapters 2, 3 and 4 grew out of our talks at the conference "The Histories of Hungarian Popular Music" held at the Institute for Musicology of the Hungarian Academy of Sciences in Budapest in March 2019. Thank you, Ádám Ignácz and Anna Dalos of the Department of 20th and 21st Century Hungarian Music for organizing it so that we could build on all the lively conversations and helpful remarks received there. Chapter 5 was based on Anna's talk for the conference section of the MusicaFemina International Symposium, also held in Budapest, at the Central European University, January 8–9, 2020. We are grateful furthermore to György Böhm for an important interview, András D. Hajdú and Éva Domonyi for using their photos, and Titusz Fábián for digging out an intriguing quote from Tibor Polgár.

Edit András, Pál Réti, György C. Kálmán, Krisztina Márkus, Ági Bori Mottern, and András Gruber helped improve on various versions of the chapters with their attentive reading and commentary. Nora Gruber, thank you for your superb help with the visual illustrations. Aron Gruber, your genuine curiosity about the progress of this project mattered a great deal. Orsolya Kálmán, Áron and Barnabás Rónai kept András's spirit as high as possible throughout writing this book.

Preface

A Conversation Between the Authors

Anna Szemere (AS)   Bea Palya belongs to the most intriguing and acclaimed popular musical artists in contemporary Hungary. During her career, which spans more than two decades, she has co-composed and performed her songs with top-notch local musicians in jazz, traditional, and classical music who, were it not for Palya's projects, wouldn't find themselves collaborating on the same stage! She has released fifteen solo albums, toured internationally, and appeared in films.[1] Given her proclivity to cross boundaries, she commands a bewildering range of genres and styles, from traditional musical idioms (Hungarian, Indian, Middle Eastern, Bulgarian) to jazz, blues, classical contemporary, and pop. Her unique retro album co-produced with Samu Gryllus *Én leszek a játékszered* (I'll Be Your Plaything) displays a richness of musical invention and a sardonic wit in invoking some of the most memorable songs of Cold War-era Hungary, which, with its critical approach to gender issues, inspired us to scrutinize it in more depth for this volume.

---

[1] See Palya's official website http://www.palyabea.hu/en/bio; for her screen appearances, see https://www.imdb.com/name/nm1847254/.

András Rónai (AR)   Listening to "I'll Be Your Plaything" for the first time was an epiphany for me, bringing to mind another epiphany two years previous. In 2008, the organizers of the annual, week-long Sziget Festival and Gábor Presser, one of the greats of Hungarian pop and rock, held a press conference addressing the "alarming state of the Hungarian song,"[2] as fewer and fewer Hungarian songs were intimately known to the listening public. (What they failed to note was that their imagined Golden Age when everyone could hum Hungarian songs had been the effect of the centralized socialist media ecosystem controlled by the party-state!) To remedy this problem, they organized The Day of the Hungarian Song, first on Sziget, and later across the country.

So there I was, a music critic, at this event of the Sziget Festival, where dozens of Hungarian pop and rock icons of the previous decades showed up performing, in quick succession, two or three of their old hits. Their goal was to entertain with an appeal to nostalgia and have the crowd sing along. The show was dragging on for seven endless hours and my professional duties didn't allow me to escape. (Embarrassingly, the audience members seemed to remember the lyrics better than some of the performers!) At about two-thirds into this atrocious and musically unrewarding sequence of performances, an ad hoc supergroup called Rock Allstars came forward with a song called *Tinédzser Dal* (Teenagers' Song), originally performed by the hard rock outfit *Dinamit* (Dynamite) back in 1979. I never really cared about the rock music of the era (I was a toddler at the time of hard rock's heyday), so the silliness of this song's lyrics stunned me.

Preface

---

[2]On the Sziget Festival, see Szemere and Nagy (2017).

AS Let me digress momentarily from your story to offer a footnote to this chapter of the Hungarian rock story. In the youth cultural lingo of the 1970s the "sincere and hard-as-a-rock" music was associated with the anti-regime sentiments and frustration of working class, disgruntled and runaway teens from the housing projects of socialist cities. This subculture appeared as a threat to the communist authorities, especially when bohemian intellectuals had discovered them for their various literary and musical projects. These heavy rock bands grew immensely popular, yet were disfavored by the media (Kőbányai 1979, Horváth 2009). They produced powerful and poignant songs, as well as embarrassingly poor ones.

AR Indeed. So the chorus went like this: "Sons of the underpass/your fate is *somewhat* broken." The word "somewhat" (*valahol*) is a typical filler for third-rate lyricists to produce the right number of syllables. It also undermines the song's somber tone completely. Lines like "I don't bring snacks to school/ Someone will have one/I'll ask to share that" just added to the unintended comic effect.

AS I'd like to note that, although girls were far from absent in the underpasses or as fans of bands such as Piramis, Beatrice, or V'Motorock, the often lambasted sexist bias of rock can all too easily be pinpointed here in the use of "sons" in the quoted line, rendering the daughters invisible.

AR Dinamit was as male chauvinist as most other heavy rock bands, but they were pooh-poohed by many as a "state-made rock group" [*állami rockzenekar*], that is, produced and promoted by apparatchiki in the music business keen to create tamed and easily manipulatable rock stars for a growing mass of alienated youth, "the sons of the underpass." Meanwhile, the more credible bands, perceived subversive, became sidelined. The label "state-made" stuck to Dinamit and eventually led to its demise. Its front man, Gyula Vikidál, also a member of the Rock Allstars supergroup, was later revealed to have been an informant.

AS And yet not even three decades of drastic social change and the discrediting information on the band could ruin the allure of Teenagers' Song for former fans!

AR Precisely. This song was bogus from the start, and I asked myself, shouldn't it be obvious to everyone in 2008 how blatantly it lied? Looking around in the audience, I was astounded by the large number of the by then middle aged and comfortably middle class fans who waxed nostalgic, while mouthing each word along with Mr. Vikidál. But I couldn't blame any of those fans for what seemed to be a genuine reaction to a song evoking their past. It was the musical symbol of their youth.

AS "Nostalgia is so certain," writes Carrie Brownstein, actress and musician in the all-female US indie band, Sleater-Kinney, "the sense of familiarity it instills makes us feel like we know ourselves, like we've lived. To get a sense that we have already journeyed through something—survived it, experienced it— is often so much easier and less messy than the task of currently live through something" (2015: 4). Although Brownstein offers insight as to why even flawed musical artifacts from our past hold a grip on us, one may go further to ask, "What if our personal and collective past only *seems* less messy than the present? What if it is no less difficult to grapple with than our present issues"? But let's not run too much ahead.

A growing literature on the relationship between memory and music testifies to the powerful role music plays in our lives as containers of memory (e.g. DeNora 2000, Istvandity 2014). Our past musical experiences become so powerfully attached to significant scenes, persons, causes, or even traumas of a specific stage in our life story, that they effectively serve as building blocks of who we become, in other words, of our personal identity. On the social psychological level, at least, we can explain why on the Day of the Hungarian Song Mr. Vikidál's middle-aged fans held fast onto an untainted or innocent image of what those bands stood for, and why they as mature adults protected that adolescent experience from a sober critical revision. Yet it is possible to take a different perspective. Isn't this incident a symptom of a larger disorder in the workings of societal memory in postsocialist Hungary? Doesn't this form of nostalgia, in your view, involve some kind of ethical and intellectual laziness?

AR   Maybe, but not on a personal level; it's an inertia of the society as a whole. It is by now common wisdom that not even a radical transformation of the regime entails a thorough-going change in most people's everyday lives, their cultural habits, and outlook on the world. There are moments when such a recognition of "no-change" becomes crystallized in a particular moment through a personal experience.

AS   I understand why you felt frustration with this mindless memorialization, wanting to just run away. But shouldn't this bizarre singalong event be viewed as a symptom of an unhealthy continuity in people's everyday cultural habits and thoughts, as if 1989 hadn't happened? What if, looking back, these fans, as Brownstein's comment suggests, found more sense and meaning in their teenage lives than their present realities? Or, what if their apparent dismissal of the Kádár era's duplicity and repression of youth culture resulted from their disillusionment with postsocialist change with its myriad social and political problems?[3] The fascinating documentary *East Punk Memories* made by the French filmmaker Lucile Chaufour about socialist-era Hungarian punk bands reflecting on their past and present lives twenty years later, gives credence to the perception of widespread disaffection. In the formulation of Dina Iordanova, historian of East European cinema, "the most radical social change of the end of the tumultuous twentieth century, a soft revolution that was undertaken with a vision of renewal, reinvigoration, and reinvention of a social order, failed to deliver. It descended into economic volatility, precariousness, and massive outmigration" (2012: 18).

AR   That diagnosis contains some truth, but only a partial one. It depicts a cycle whereby socialism was followed by failed capitalism spawning nostalgia for socialism. Yet in some aspects of our lives, we see an almost total inertia, for example, in our rigidly centralized and ideologically driven educational system, which I experience daily through my school-age sons. Meanwhile, people continue to welcome rapid changes in technology-driven consumer and media culture.

---

[3] János Kádár (1912–1989) was the General Secretary of the Hungarian Socialist Workers' Party from 1956 until his retirement in 1988. He died in the year when his party conceded its power to a set of oppositional parties. As the first leader after the crackdown of the 1956 revolution by the Soviets, Kádár was instrumental in the harsh retaliations (including the execution of the reigning prime minister Imre Nagy), but soon achieved popularity by establishing a soft dictatorship nicknamed "Goulash socialism," which involved a measure of economic well-being, cultural permissiveness, and relative autonomy in citizens' private life.

But let me return to the Day of the Hungarian Song. Being around former fans of "sincere rock" so deeply connecting with a poetically flawed, silly, and deeply dishonest song decades later, made me conscious of the need for cultural change through a profound critical assessment of the socialist past and its popular culture. Not just its songs, but its movies, television, and everyday objects would need to be re-examined so that we can respond to or enjoy them in a new fashion. This train of thought is where Bea Palya's album "I'll Be Your Plaything" fits in. If the reception of "Teenagers' Song" by Dinamit was deeply disturbing, a sad epiphany about misapprehending the collective past, listening to *this* album was mesmerizing, a cheerful epiphany. This is the way musical remembering should be, I thought. Reflecting on the past decades and uncovering hitherto unseen meanings in its popular culture doesn't need to be a painful process. On the contrary, it can be funny, playful, liberating, and empowering.

AS   For me too, it was a revelation to hear the album. As someone spending most of her time in the United States, I wondered how such a spirited and innovative musical project had evaded my attention! Although, on the surface, "I'll Be Your Plaything" appears as yet another retro album digging back to Cold War-era oldies, Palya, Gryllus, and their ensemble created a politically and musically sophisticated concept album. Its backbone comprises covers of the winning songs of the annually held Dance Song Festival [*Táncdalfesztivál*] of Kadarist Hungary where old-style *estrada*-type music squared off with the fresh Anglo-American sounds of beat music.[4] In reinterpreting

---

[4]The term's origin is French (*estrade*), referring to a stage for performances. It also means live entertainment art similar to vaudeville, including singing, dance, circus on stage, illusionism, parody, and clownery. In the Soviet Union and its satellites, from Mongolia to the German Democratic Republic during

these songs, freely hybridizing musical genres and idioms, often to hilarious effect, wielding humor, nostalgic sentiment, and scathing satire, Palya and her ensemble conveyed their distinctive (and gendered!) generational perspective, while showing us listeners the world of older generations in the fun-house mirror of boldly rearranged tunes.

AR   In the two decades after the regime changes of Central and Eastern Europe, countless articles and books have addressed the need to "come to terms with the past," and how such a reflection failed to take place in earnest. Memory discourse in Hungary has largely focused on the narrowly defined political sphere, giving the impression that facing the past cannot be anything but painful, even though occasionally cathartic.[5] But with Palya's and Gryllus's project a wholly different approach emerged.

AS   Since the album was released in 2010, the right-wing conservative Fidesz party with its increasingly autocratic leader, Viktor Orbán, has been re-elected three times and even become the most notorious populist in the European Union.

---

the Cold War estrada was a generic term for a conservative style of popular musical entertainment regulated by the state. Estrada had its superstars (Iosif Kobzon, Alla Pugachova, Karel Gott) along with credentialed and salaried ensembles of musicians.

[5]An important exception to this hiatus has been literary prose and drama where memory work started in the late socialist era. Péter Nádas's *The End of a Family Story* (Egy családregény vége, 1977) and *Világló részletek* (Illuminating parts, 2017), Péter Esterházy's *Celestial Harmonies: A Novel* (Harmonia Caelestis, 2000, 2004) and *Javított kiadás* (Revised edition, 2002), Géza Bereményi's *Magyar Copperfield* (Hungarian Copperfield 2020), Miklós Vámos's *The Book of Fathers* (Apák könyve, 2006) and Pál Závada's *Egy piaci nap* (A day at the farmer's market, 2016) are but the most renowned examples of this type of deep drilling into personal and collective pasts.

As we assess the status and value of Palya's album, we can't help but reflect on its commentary on state socialism at a time when Orbán's regime frequently invites parallels between the two kinds of societies.

AR   It's been argued that this government could strip away so many freedoms won after the regime change without potent resistance only because entrenched beliefs and habits of the socialist era have survived in our society. For example, in 2019, an article in the opposition weekly *Hvg* (Weekly World Economy) asked "Why are we still the people of Kádár"? In it, social scientists questioned if it is in the DNA of Hungarians to prioritize their modest, material well-being over personal freedoms and democratic values. As well, they pointed to the deep historical roots of twenty-first century authoritarianism in Hungary. As a resident of Budapest whose everyday life is powerfully shaped by these realities, I am inclined not merely to ask the question, "How could we have ended up like this"? but to wonder what would have happened in our society and culture if this delightful, yet far from uncritical, take on the socialist past as exemplified by "I'll Be Your Plaything" had become more widespread and resonant in Hungarian pop culture?

AS   There is no straightforward answer to your questions. Yet we both believe that pop culture is of political consequence and, at its best, can boost societal immunity to the current regime's far too successful efforts to revive the worst aspects of state socialism: its inward-looking, conservative, and authoritarian tendencies.

*   *   *

AS   When disclosing to my American friends that I was co-writing a book about a Hungarian popular-musical album, they responded enthusiastically but added: "Too bad that I won't be able to read it." "Why not"? I asked. "Because you must be writing it in Hungarian." Their assumption revealed something rather disheartening about the global status of popular music in a small, semi-peripheral country such as Hungary. It implies, why would anybody but Hungarians care about an exemplar of Hungarian popular music? Indeed, because of its geopolitical position and decades-long (relative) isolation during the twentieth century from the global popular music business, Hungary, similarly to other countries in this region, has produced few international stars. Budapest has raised its popular musical profile with the aforementioned Sziget Festival, but few foreigners have been lured by the local musical offerings (even if they may well discover some during their stay at the festival). Consumers and practitioners of folk and "world music" are surely familiar with the singer Márta Sebestyén or the ensemble Muzsikás. Some blues aficionados might even know that Little G Weevil, one of the world's most renowned traditional blues players, is Hungarian born as Gábor Szűcs, as was the late jazz guitarist Gábor Szabó.

However, we were looking for music not only worth listening to for its aesthetic qualities, but that is contemporary sounding and uses local musical idioms, which in turn would offer us an excuse to explore a few hot button issues of modern Hungarian society, such as the politics of femininity, ethnic "otherness," collective, and personal remembrance of the past regime and more.

On February 13 2020, we recorded a marathon-long interview with Palya and Gryllus in Budapest. András had known both of them in person, had interviewed Bea for magazine articles over the years, and even published a remarkable study about her (Rónai 2017). I had never met Bea before but had collaborated with Samu in organizing a conference adjacent to that year's MusicaFemina International Symposium held in Budapest.[6] Our interview had a lively informal atmosphere. And when working with the recorded interview, we were captivated by the joyful and spirited manner in which Bea and Samu remembered so many details of making the album ten years earlier, as well as the various episodes of their shared history as musical collaborators. This gave us the idea for Chapter 1, to explore the cultural significance of play and its interconnectedness with music, not only regarding the album itself (whose title is a play on a song title that includes the word "plaything") but also regarding the nature of Bea and Samu's unique relationship and earlier work together.

The album came out twenty-one years after the collapse of state socialism, a time period in Hungarian history sent to oblivion rather abruptly. Cultural memories of socialism became politicized as well as commodified. Why and how did the Dance Song Festival and its winning songs matter for Hungarians young and old? We seek to answer this question in Chapter 2 by enlisting theories of collective memory and music as a medium preeminently suited to reflect on public and personal pasts. Chapter 3 places postsocialist nostalgia in the broader context of "posts'" of the 2000s, most notably, of the global trends of retromania and hauntology. We argue, with help from theories such as dialogism and actor-network theory, that conversing with the past through covers has more

<hr>

[6]MusicaFemina International Symposium convenes annually to offer a multimedia platform for researchers, music professionals, and local communities in Central and Eastern Europe to explore relations of gender and musical practice.

to it than cheap nostalgia, and may be a vehicle for producing new sounds and meanings. Chapter 4 focuses on the design of "I'll Be Your Plaything" as a cover album with an avant-gardist concept that incorporates and comments on traces ("found objects") from everyday life of the 1960s. Chapters 5 and 6 dwell on the politics of gender and popular feminism as a long-running theme in Bea's creative output. Chapter 5 describes the hurdles Bea has faced in the music business to become a singer-songwriter, and examines her manner of engagement with popular feminist themes in "I'll Be Your Plaything." The aim of Chapter 6 is to demonstrate the ongoing and increasingly profound address of womanhood in Bea's musical trajectory over the past ten years.

1 Playing Music, Playing with Music: Bea Palya and Samu Gryllus's Musical Partnerships

Can you imagine hearing Dusty Springfield's romantic pop hit "You Don't Have to Say You Love Me" rearranged with Arabic instruments such as ouds, tabla, and kawalas? How about Celine Dion's megahit "My Heart Will Go On" (the love theme from the blockbuster *Titanic*) performed with a completely different chord set so as to baffle the listener every time the resolution of a long-building narrative tension is missed or hijacked? Finally, would you be intrigued to hear, say, the melody of Carole King's perennial "You've Got a Friend" sung with inflections and melismas characteristic of Roma (Gypsy)/Balkan folk singing?[1] Answering "yes" or "perhaps" to any of these questions means to have some inkling of the nature of the musical play Bea Palya and Samu Gryllus engaged in when selecting more than a dozen Hungarian pop hits, complemented with two global hits from the US, that they

---

[1] The term "Roma" represents the preferred but relatively recent collective term for this ethnic group, therefore it will be used in all cases except when only the term "Gypsy" (*cigány*) is appropriate, such as in the genre designation *cigányzene* (music played by Roma to entertain the "non-Roma") or in contexts where the term Roma would be anachronistic.

most vividly remembered from their younger years or what they deemed most alluring to cover some twenty years later. Most of the songs were already oldies at the time. Some of them gained layers of new meaning as soundtracks to cinema or cover versions.

Gryllus remembered the recording sessions taking place amidst roaring laughs. "Never before had I been working in such an exhilarating atmosphere! It was non-stop craziness!" Palya elaborated on this, saying: "It was crazy but in the best possible sense of the word, with top-notch musicians all of whom brought their musical skills of their own genre to bear on the project. Several of them met with each other for the first time on the spot (Rónai 2010). The project pulled together professional musicians of wildly different sensibilities, experiences, and musical outlooks from jazz, folk, pop/rock, world, and classical music. Collaborators with Palya and Gryllus in earlier projects, they were cherry-picked not merely to play a specific kind of music but to play *with* music for this unique cover album. The making of the album, whose title playfully reversed the eponymous song's title 'I Won't Be Your Plaything' to 'I'll Be Your Plaything,' served, first and foremost, as a playground for us." Gryllus reflected in a recent interview. Before delving into the making and the musical features of that album, we will need to embark on a lengthy journey to address two themes crucial to it: the nature of play in and through music pertaining to Samu and Bea's collaborations (this chapter) and issues of postsocialist remembering and nostalgia relevant to the cultural and political context of "I'll Be Your Plaything" as a cover album (Chapter 2).

In his book titled *Homo Ludens*, the Dutch cultural historian, Johan Huizinga, provided a sustained argument about play as a fundamental aspect of cultures across history. Being a close kin to jest, laughter, wit, and the comic, on the one hand, and to rituals and contests, on the other, play, in his definition, "is a voluntary activity or occupation executed within certain fixed limits of time and place, according to rules freely accepted but absolutely binding, having its aim in itself and accompanied by a feeling of tension, joy, and the consciousness that it is 'different' from 'ordinary' life" (1949/1980: 28). Huizinga's theory has some critical oversights, however, most notably, his idealization of play as an act of "pure freedom" located outside of normal social life and impervious to profit interests or material gain (ibid. 8). Commoditized and often exploited by multi-billion dollar industries, most forms of play in modern capitalism—from video games to spectator sports and television contests—are deeply embedded in, and, to a degree, forged by the rules of the market and a set of regulatory systems. Nevertheless, Huizinga's emphasis on play's relative separation from, or suspense of, workaday realities, its being bound by voluntarily accepted rules or its ability to fully absorb its practitioners through joy is of paramount importance. Huizinga, moreover, pointed out a profound nexus between play and music, noting that even the manipulation of musical instruments in many languages is signified by the verb "play" (ibid. 42, 158). (The Hungarian language is one of them.) Beyond any music's intimate ties with play, however, certain forms and genres of music are distinctly play*ful,* using humor, jokes, and parody. An endless number of examples could be cited from classical to folk music, and from rock to punk and hip hop. A few randomly selected examples range from Joseph Haydn's Farewell Symphony where the sections' musicians leave the orchestra one by one to Woody Guthrie's ironic political commentary; Frank Zappa's parodies and the Beastie Boys' use of sampling to comic effect. Therefore, it is worth distinguishing between a more general sense of music-as-play from the ways intentional playfulness and humor imparts a distinct character to music—especially, to the experience of making it. It is in this latter sense that the creation of the album "I'll Be Your Plaything" seemed like a playground to the musicians. But the metaphor could aptly characterize aspects of their earlier work together, which we will outline in the remaining part of this chapter.

1.1. Coming of Age Together: The Early Years of Musical Collaboration

Playing with music is more effortless when musicians can boast of a history of a special friendship and musical partnership. Samu and Bea met before they were twenty, in the mid-1990s, when participating in an offbeat music group named Laokoón, led by Samu himself. This is how Bea remembers the peculiar character of the group:

> Samu surrounded himself with all kinds of cool misfits, including myself, so that we could play our polyphonic compositions, study together Indian music, minimalism, [Western] classical and folk musics, explore modal scales, repetitions, the relationship between music and theater, songwriting, the concepts of time … and silence.
>
> Palya 2011: 210

Laokoón's scope included a range of musical genres and other art forms, while its members also traced art to its cultural and historical roots and contexts. Discussions of Indian music and John Cage led to talks about world religions and vegetarianism, and appreciation of Hungarian poetry to modes of vocal production. Laokoón didn't refrain from giving serious thought to popular music either, whether mainstream Hungarian pop, American rock, or a Bulgarian soccer anthem. A sense of quirkiness was no less prevalent than high-brow intellectualism at its gatherings. Sponsored by a grant from George Soros, the group rehearsed four times a week and performed a new program every month. But for about a dozen young talents, it primarily served as a vehicle and a site of musical maturation, learning, hilarity, and social bonding (Palya 2011: 209–14; Lange 2018: 59–60). In the wake of Laokoón's dissolution, Palya and Gryllus sustained their friendship and collaboration over the years. Regarding each other as brother and sister—at times even twins!—they complemented, challenged, inspired, and critiqued each other, even while their careers and personal lives landed them far apart. Born in 1976, they represented the first generation to have come of age in post Cold War Hungary, with opportunities to tour, study, and weave personal and professional relationships in Europe and America.

Samu, a versatile and erudite musician-composer engaged, primarily, in jazz and new music, came from a family of legendary musicians. His father, Dániel, and uncle, Vilmos, founded the group Kaláka in 1969, which hasn't ceased to feed generations of audiences, including, but not exclusively, young people, with songs inspired by classic and contemporary poetry and a wide range of folk idioms. Kaláka has developed a language of its own replete with musical humor and poetic play. The extended Gryllus family offered a culturally vibrant and nurturing second home in Budapest to the young Bea, who grew up in a village called Bag into a low-income working class family. An outstanding student, she was selected to study in an elite high school in the capital and, upon completion, she stayed in Budapest to obtain her college degree in ethnography and pursue a career as a singer. As invaluable as the "Gryllus-house" was for Bea in regard to her aesthetic horizon and self-confidence, she in turn brought her down-to-earth experience of village life and culture to bear on their friendship and collaborations. At six, she started singing and dancing in the preservationist folk ensemble of Bag. "It was the old women dancers who brushed our hair and helped us put on our wide skirts. Not only did we learn the dances and the songs from them but also the stamina," Palya recalls in her memoir (2011: 20–1). For many years, her grandmother prepared her bridal wreath to perform the role of a bride in a staged village wedding. But when Bea's teacher gave her an ethnomusicological recording of an old folk song on a cassette tape to study, she was embarrassed to not be able to listen to it at home since they did not own a cassette player (ibid.). In the Hungary of the 1980s, even for a village girl, this level of poverty was embarrassing to reveal to a teacher! Besides, the music of choice in her home was not respectable "authentic," folk but the massively popular *magyarnóta* (folk-like urban song), dismissed as kitsch by the educated elite. Bea's maternal grandfather, a Romani man she affectionately called "Tata" (old dad), who loved to sing, caused Bea to embrace aspects of this ethnic heritage not only through studying Romani folk singing but through fashioning a more outspoken, feisty persona associated with "Gypsy" women in the European imaginary. She no doubt risked alienating some segments of her audience and potential sponsors in this way, although this knowledge served as cultural capital in her quest to enter world music markets and become recognized in Budapest's highly selective urbane elite.

Romani folk enthused Palya about a range of other ethnic sounds and singing techniques, and Gryllus was a congenial companion in this exploration. In her words, "[Samu] took me to numerous concerts such as those of the Calcutta Trio, showed me new things, not just folk music that, he said, I could benefit from studying..." (ibid. 211). He gave serious attention and encouragement to Bea's ideas and initiatives. Not that she was unaware of her own strengths, most notably, her mastery of folk music. Bea had been performing and recording albums with folk and world music ensembles, such as Zurgó, Kárpátia, and Folkestra. Her first solo album *Ágról Ágra* (From Branch to Branch) featuring Hungarian, Gypsy, Romanian, Bulgarian, and Persian songs came out in 2003. She lived and studied Indian music in Paris, and formed her own Bea Palya Quintet in 2005.

During the 2000s, Gryllus obtained a Master's degree in Media Composition from the University of Music and Performing Arts, Vienna, after which, with the support of an Erasmus scholarship, he focused on composition and experimental music-theater at the University of Arts in Berlin. He became a Fulbright Scholar at Wesleyan University, Connecticut, in 2008/2009, working with Alvin Lucier, Anthony Braxton, and Ron Kuivila. Not only did Gryllus and Palya have a chance as musical artists to study and spend extended periods of time abroad, their respective careers benefited from a cosmopolitan lifestyle. Strolling in the streets of Budapest or Moscow, New York, Berlin, or Vienna, Palya relates, "in the morning or at night, during the summer or winter, we could always quickly tune in our shared 'SamuBea world'—a shared wavelength that was unique and special to them and talk, listen, and laugh, while exchanging creative ideas and plans" (ibid. 214). Their contrasting personalities proved fruitful to their creative efforts. Bea saw Samu as analytical, meticulous, and somewhat detached, as opposed to her more instinctive and hot-blooded self. Crucially, they shared a joie de vivre, self-effacing humor, and an open-minded artistry. As well, they searched and seized opportunities for joint projects.

Palya's second solo album, *Álom, álom, kitalálom* was co-created with Gryllus and Mátyás Bólya, a folk multi-instrumentalist.[2] Drawing on folk symbolism, it featured Hungarian, Romani, and Bengali folk songs, tales, and poetry. With children being its primary audience, the album had a humorous layer to it, in the true spirit of the Kaláka tradition. "Recalling our collaboration," Bea writes, "what comes to mind are bright and cheery afternoons, sitting in Mátyás's living room, replaying a tune the umpteenth time and sinking our heads into Samu's music sheets. Mátyás's toddler is crawling on the floor stuffing toys into her mouth. Each time when she loves a musical segment, she looks up at us [...] and breaks into bubbly laughter! In this way we could immediately test what would or wouldn't work for kids"! (ibid. 218). *Álom, álom* was Bea's first album for which she authored the story, along with the songs' melodies and lyrics (with Samu's arrangement), marking a significant point in her career as a songwriter. The storyline revolved around a young woman seeking her voice and romantic love as she navigates the world of dreams and realities. The music was later set to stage by puppeteers and dance troupes.

1.2. Graduating with *Psyché*

The next project was setting music to Sándor Weöres's *Psyché* (1972), an instant classic of twentieth-century Hungarian

---

[2]The title is an untranslatable word play. *Álom* means "dream" and the rhyming word *kitalálom* could be translated as "I'm figuring out." The phrase refers to the protagonist's willingness to learn deeper truths about herself by exploring her dreams. The phrase furthermore connotes Hungarian Romani (Vlach) folk poetry where "álom, álom" is a recurrent nonsensical interjection similar to "shoobie doobie" in American jazz.

literature. Its heroine, Erzsébet Lónyay, is the fictional nineteenth-century author of poetry complemented by Weöres with biographies and diary fragments. A free-spirited young woman with half-Romani ancestry, Lónyay lives a short, yet adventurous life abounding in sexual escapades, high-society splendor, and brutal mistreatment.

Both Bea and Samu had an abiding fascination with *Psyché*. She, as a teenager, composed melodies to some of "her" poems. "I was stunned to read about a woman so much like me," she reflects. "I got both excited and relieved—yes, I knew how she felt, only that I couldn't articulate them so well! I merged with Lónyay" (Palya 2011: 226). Like herself, Lónyay was also an ethnic "other," endowed with remarkable artistic talents, and experiencing wildly diverse—lower and upper class—social milieus from childhood to adulthood. Someone who struggled with complexes as a village girl thrown into an elite social world, Bea could easily empathize with an exoticized nineteenth-century Gypsy poetess who, like herself, never felt secure among her admirers. Despite being the brainchild of a male poet, the artistic and rebellious poetess proved so vibrant and real to Bea that "she" urged her "to revisit existential questions concerning death, life, woman, man, love and soul … and the difficulties of being creative" (ibid. 228). She questioned how Psyché's story would enable, her, a twenty-first century singer-songwriter, to develop a musical career with authenticity and dignity, and without being derailed by others' judgement. In relishing Lónyay's poems, Bea became enamored with their actual author as well, confessing that, "I went to bed and woke up with the cassette where [Weöres] recited his own poems" as " [it] purged the dark demons from me" (ibid.).

Psyché had an allure for Samu as well, dating back to his high school years. He grew up surrounded by Weöres's tomes on the family's bookshelves. Weöres's poetry has resulted in some of the best-known Kaláka songs. Kaláka even made a habit of visiting the author in his home to showcase its musical arrangements to his poems, and in return, received signed copies from him. When traveling to study composition in Berlin, Samu took but a handful of books with him. One of them was *Psyché*. In the two young artists' imaginations, Weöres possessed superhuman power. "When some problem—legal, technical or musical—suddenly got resolved," Samu explained, "we figured him as an angel perched on the clouds taking good care of us."[3]

The thrust of the creative work, according to Bea, rested on the network of four "actors": Gryllus and herself, the late poet's mystical presence as well as his charismatic creature, Erzsébet Lónyay. It appears that a complicated psychodynamic of identifications was at work involving Palya's subjectivity merging with Lónyay's, and her love affair with a supernatural storyteller. By virtue of engaging creatively with Weöres's piece, Bea's "twin brother," Samu, faced a Freudian challenge. As son and nephew of the elder Grylluses, he was to emulate their musical accomplishments in Kaláka, but also to prove himself as the student or follower of such internationally acclaimed composers as György Ligeti and Péter Eötvös, both of whom have set music to Weöres-texts. In addition, it was Samu's father, Dániel, commissioning the new *Psyché* adaptation for Hangzó Helikon, a series co-produced by his record label, Gryllus Ltd and the book publisher Helikon. Bea's memories bear witness to the daunting task ahead: "There we stood, Samu and myself, in front of this towering masterpiece, green at thirty, as we thrust ourselves into it. Weren't we courageous?

---

[3]E-mail communication, April 16, 2020.

Sure we were, but fearful, too"! (ibid. 226). Further, she describes evocatively the dialectic of the creative process: "*Psyché* is formidable! And [like Lónyay], Samu and me also died of the poems, but then revived! Isn't it an act of creation! The old folks, Sanyika [nickname for Weöres—A.S.] and his Psyché produced *us* but we were also producing *them* (italics by me, A.S.). As many metamorphoses and mutual birthing as the lines connecting the four of us!" (ibid. 227).

Psyché relies on old Hungarian and Romani folk songs as its main musical material, yet it is a complex piece of contemporary art music where instrumentation and melodic leitmotifs symbolize aspects of the heroine's life story, thoughts, and sentiments. Its compositional sources and techniques match up with the sophistication and historicism of the literary original, despite its shortened narrative (Németh 2016, Lange 2018: 63–5). Samu was in charge of the architecture and the engineering of the final sound of the album, while Bea brought her melodies to some poems, and several segments were born out of collective improvisations by the Quintet. The versification of some songs, such as the climactic fifteen-minute-long "Epistola ennen magamhoz" (Epistle to Myself), inspired Palya to use Arab singing techniques, enabling her to alternate between chanting, exclamations, and ornate melodious singing.

Psyché, the album and its ensuing stage performances gained critical acclaim for the Gryllus-Palya duo (and the Quintet) from literary and art musical circles, but appealed to a larger audience as well (Lange 2018: 65–8). As a gesture of appreciation, the actress Mariann Csernus, who had recited an adaptation of Weöres' work hundreds of times on stage, gifted Bea the costume she was wearing for the role. The world music critic, László Marton Távolodó (2006) praised *Psyché* for a

Figure 1 *Bea Palya with Samu Gryllus.*

feature Bea and Samu had been least confident about in the outset, its maturity and musical language transgressing genre boundaries. Rónai emphasized the clever deployment of avant-garde musical devices along with "captivating virtuosic vocal performance and hummable melodies." As well, he suggested that *Psyché* is overwhelming, "too much," partly because "it overrides the distinct identities of the songs." This excessiveness, however, captured the heroine's main personality trait, also attributed to Palya as an artist "transgressing social norms and gender roles by 'too much' creativity, love, empathy, eroticism, and longing" (2017: 105).

Psyché became an important item on the new music composer's and the former folk singer's resume. Samu demonstrated, once again, that there was more to his fledgling career than name recognition, while Bea proved herself as a singer-songwriter subverting established genre rubrics. Not that she had abandoned folk or traditional music. She merely protested the label of folk singer, which in Hungary, especially for women, is still tied up with a specific concept of authenticity and the safeguarding of tradition as heritage. It thus offers limited freedom for revival artists for self-expression—an issue we will revisit in Chapter 5. With her album *Álom, álom*, Bea was already keen to utilize ethnic sounds and vocal styles in a more subjective, improvisatory, and eclectic manner, more in tune with a twenty-first century sensibility. *Psyché*'s success further liberated and encouraged her to continue taking that path of radically broadening the thematic scope of popular song and making room for nuanced portrayals of distinctly female experiences and ways of being in the world.

2 Memory Work with Souvenirs, Bronzes, and the Tunes of State Socialism

In her memoir, Bea evoked a special moment occurring a few years before she created the album "I'll Be Your Plaything." On a visit to her brother, she was practising the 1960s oldie "I Won't Be Your Plaything," while tending to her young nephew. Bea's mother was also around, playing with her granddaughter. She was singing along with Bea, increasing or decreasing the volume, staying in tune, and remembering every single word of the lyrics. The glasses slid down on her nose; nonetheless, Bea could suddenly see, in her aging mother, the young girl yearning for love and ecstasy while imitating the sounds of Kati Kovács, the original performer's singing.[1] The little kids also sensed their grandmother's odd metamorphosis. "I'll

---

[1] Kati Kovács (1944–) is one of the most renowned and commercially successful pop and rock singers of her native Hungary, a recipient, among others, of the highest national Kossuth Award, and winner of international music festivals. She has also dabbled in songwriting and acting. During socialism, she toured and recorded in Soviet Bloc countries while gaining some recognition in Western Europe. A mainstream artist, she pioneered rock, soul, jazz, and blues singing in Hungary and in the region.

need to work with these songs someday," Bea thought (Palya 2011: 237).

In our preface, we have touched upon how music as a mnemonic medium can evoke, with dramatic force, our personal and collective experiences—a certain phase in our life, an event, a relationship, or a situation, with all its emotional charge and sensorial qualities. Drawing on empirical studies, Lauren Istvandity explains that music serves as a receptacle of autobiographical memories, and its various elements (lyrics, arrangement, etc.) "have a capacity to embody [their] atmosphere and emotionality in ways that exceed spoken language" (2014: 19). Music moreover is mobile, and its connotations change once coupled with different artifacts (for instance as a soundtrack to an ad or a movie) or when sounded in an unusual setting (DeNora 2015: 3–4). Music's fusion, coupling with, and decoupling from, a variety of lived experiences, may give us a clue about the unique power it exerts over us, even when dismissed on aesthetic or political grounds. This feature of music also accounts for it being the preeminent medium of sparking nostalgic or difficult sentiments. Music's emotional grip on us, irrespective of its perceived value, its ability to catalyze longing after or disavowing our past, is of particular relevance in addressing Hungary's transition period in the wake of the regime change, when the collective dynamic of remembering and forgetting intersected with people's individual biographies in myriad ways. Bea and Simu's album covering socialist era pop songs two decades into postsocialism, cannot be fully appreciated without the broader political context and practices of public memory.

2.1. "Let's Make a Clean Slate of the Past"! And the Pop-culturization of Memories

When the Berlin Wall fell, a plethora of objects, images, and songs associated with state socialism flooded the consumer markets of Central and Eastern Europe. The symbolism, sentiments, and memory practices spawned an extensive journalistic and academic discourse on nostalgia and collective memory.[2] In Hungary, one of the most memorable commodities was an empty can of liverwurst with a new sign: "The last breath of communism." This "souvenir" conveyed a similar sense of complacence, mockery, and glee as the initial ritual of deposing statues of socialism's heroes from their pedestals and collectively hauling them to an open-air exhibit called the Memento (or Statue) Park on the outskirts of Budapest.[3] "The last breath of communism," first displayed in Memento Park, and the ghettoization of the statues, signified the new political elite's desire of the impossible, to dislodge an entire era from collective public memory. Within months, thousands of statues and old street names vanished from the prominent locales of postsocialist cities, to be replaced with those of politicians, heroes, and other iconic figures of the pre-socialist

---

[2]On memory practices in the Central and Eastern European context, we have found the works by Svetlana Boym (2001), Maria Todorova and Zsuzsa Gille (ed. 2010), Edit András (2008/2009), and Sabina Mihelj (2017) particularly useful.
[3]"The last breath of communism" (http://www.mementopark.hu/) bears the influence of Piero Manzoni's conceptualist artwork "The Artists Shit" from 1961 (https://www.wikiart.org/en/piero-manzoni/artist-s-shit-1961, last accessed February 14, 2021).

eras.[4] "Because political order," the anthropologist Katherine Verdery explains, "has something to do with both landscape and history, changing the political order, no matter where, often means changing the bronzed human beings who both stabilize the landscape and temporally freeze particular values in it" (1999: 6). Even more momentous, Verdery argues, were the ceremonies associated with the repatriation and reburial of the remains of famous dead men—emigrants and exiles—that the new regimes all across the former Soviet Bloc reclaimed as their own. The reburial of Imre Nagy, the martyred prime minister of the 1956 revolution, stood out as the most cathartic event of Hungary's transition to democracy. In contrast, the "homecoming" of the remains of Admiral Miklós Horthy, Hungary's governor between 1920 and 1944, was viewed by many as the rehabilitation of his authoritarian fascist-friendly legacy. Indeed, the political life of so many dead bodies, bronzed or skeletal, marked an admittedly morbid yet characteristic facet of postsocialist transitions.

While politicians were fervently rewriting, amidst fierce debates, the state socialist canons of national history, the era's pop culture—popular music, consumer brands, commercials, movies—seeped in to take care of memory work regarding the recent past. Before long, the successor of the socialist record company Hungaroton's pop music label, Gong, released a compilation of revolutionary songs with an English language title *Best of Communism,* on two cassette tapes and, subsequently, on CDs. The album's creator, Ákos Réthly, also

---

[4]Some would question whether the statues' removal to Statue Park as objects of touristic and/or historical interest is of identical order of intervention into public memory as the changing of street names. Whereas the former is an act of museumization, the latter is one of erasure; both, however, involve a drastic reorganization of the symbolic order.

the Statue Park's director, played the songs as ambience at the exhibit, which made so much buzz that he decided to compile and publish them as an album (Jordan 1999). But music as a cultural text works differently from the objects in urban, public spaces. Statues of a country's "greats" are static and communicate sublime messages in a straightforward manner. (Unless they are moved from their designated spot to a space like the Memento Park!) No double entendres or ironic commentaries are contained in the object itself. In contrast, music, owing to its capacity to suffuse personal and collective experiences, can convey a range of different, both individuated and collective, messages and sentiments, frequently unintended ones. In addition, music's shifting listening contexts over time, historical and biographical, also modifies its perception, meaning, and affect.

Another difference between various media of memorialization is that, once a historical figure's statue is taken down or replaced by someone else's, the site will have changed permanently. People are left with no recourse to the earlier sight, although an artefact may survive its physical existence in urban remembrance.[5] Musical artefacts overall resist erasure

---

[5]An example is the enormous statue to commemorate the death of Ilya Ostapenko, the Red Army officer who, during the siege of Budapest in December 1944, was shot by the fighters of the German Army as he approached them to hand over the Soviets' ultimatum demanding surrender. The statue was erected in 1951, demolished, like so many other Soviet monuments, during Hungary's uprising of 1956, and once again reinstated soon after the restoration of the regime by János Kádár. Standing right by the entrance to the highway connecting the capital city with Lake Balaton, "Ostapenko" became a favored meeting place for hitchhikers and other vacationers. Four years after the fall of the Berlin Wall, the statue was once again removed and hauled to Memento Park, but the spot continues to bear his name in colloquial language. Even a McDonald's restaurant that opened on that spot adopted the name Ostapenko—not in honor of the Red Army officer but to distinguish itself from another "Meki" (McDonald's local nickname) nearby. See Hofmeister (2017).

from public and personal, physical and memory archives, and may be retrieved with relative ease, and even be sounded virtually anywhere, any time by anyone.

The songs presented in *Best of Communism* did not fit the conventional sense of the term "popular." Even though some of them were craftily composed by classically trained and even outstanding composers, such as Hanns Eisler, the communist disciple of Arnold Schoenberg, most songs came across as pompous and kitschy, which of course was far from a purely aesthetic perception; they were maidservants of regimentation and indoctrination. The typical formula included references to the past as a time of class oppression and hardship set in minor key. The present, set in major key, was portrayed as a time of liberation, yet one demanding a continuous fight for peace and progress leading, as Marxist teleology held, to the radiant future. Liked or loathed, these tunes were etched into people's minds no less forcefully than their favorite pop songs. Marches and labor movement songs were routinely blasted through the airwaves or loudspeakers on official holidays; reception ceremonies held for foreign visitors; at the initiation of pioneers, draftees, or at the funerals of cadres. Not only did this repertory offer a persistent soundscape to people's lives during the regime's forty years, especially during its earlier phase in the 1950s, Hungarians actually performed them in school, in trade union and military choirs, or marched to them on May Day celebrations. Some folks did so willingly, even enthusiastically, many others reluctantly or with aversion. Already back then, however, labor movement songs served multiple functions and worked differently for various musical actors and listeners. In a literal sense, the music was called upon for action, it also prompted an older generation of Hungarians to recall their lives as prewar movement activists singing these songs in exile abroad or underground in Hungary where the Communist Party had been outlawed. Remembrance, in this case, evidently, spurred reflection on the drastically altered contexts, meanings, and uses of these songs across borders and social orders.

The album's opening track is the *International*, the anthem of the organized left and the Soviet Union's national anthem until 1944. In state socialist Hungary, the *International* accompanied the performance of the country's national anthem, signifying fealty to the military, economic, and ideological bloc headed by the Soviet Union. The song's lyrics include the principal imperative: "*Let's make a clean slate of the past,*" followed by the prophetic statement: *"The world's foundation will change,* We are nothing, now let's be all"! (italics by A.S.).[6] Svetlana Boym offers a vision of the twentieth century beginning with utopia and ending with nostalgia (2007:7). Topping the list of movement songs on the album, the *International* as the musical emblem of utopia that turned into an object of nostalgia, is particularly ironic. It demonstrates cycles of sameness and repetition in the region's history, where dramatic change was proclaimed to have happened. In reaction to postsocialist forgetting, the International reminded its listeners of the even more sweeping program of forgetting implied in the revolutionary dictum: "let's make a clean slate of

---

[6]This English language version is the literal translation of the French original written by Eugène Pottier in 1871, following the collapse of the French Commune. Interestingly, the other two English adaptations published on this site have softened the revolutionary fervor of Pottier's lyrics by stating "We'll change henceforth *the old tradition.* And spurn the dust to win the prize" (italics by me—A.S.). The Hungarian translation, however, has faithfully retained the radical, even totalitarian flavor of the International. The music was composed by Pierre De Geyter. "The International " in Marxists Internet Archive, https://www.marxists.org/history/ussr/sounds/lyrics/international.htm (last accessed February 14, 2021).

the past." Did the producers and consumers of the album identify a parallel here? Did they suggest that the postsocialist democratic cleanup of the previous order in a sense replicated the communist predecessor's urge to break with *their* past? To illustrate this point, the generation born before World War Two experienced the removal of street names and statues glorifying the Horthy era's notables, and their replacement with the names of communist notables, only to be followed by the return of the Horthyist names and statues. Could it be that underneath the democratic façade of postsocialist memory politics a historically familiar pattern of repression survived?

Were people aware of the irony involved in the recurrent symbolic cleanups in Hungary's modern history? Réthly, the album's producer, must have been framing as he did this collection of songs with the English language pop formula: "Best of …," turning these militantly anticapitalist songs into commodities in Hungary's newly globalized music business. These movement songs were compiled, repackaged, and marketed to compete with music genres they had never been in close proximity with: the "bests" of international pop-rock stars, classical music's great masters, and local hitmakers as if to illustrate Theodor Adorno's thesis regarding the relentless standardization and commoditization of everything by the capitalist culture industry.

Tapping into an emergent wave of nostalgia after the socialist past, *Best of Communism* was among the hottest-selling CDs in the year of its release, and even the prospect of exporting it to the United States seemed plausible (Jordan, ibid). It joined a range of pop-culturized items to find a market among locals and tourists alike. Listeners, apparently, resonated with *Best of Communism* in multiple ways—and have continued to do so ever since—even as this genre now inhabits an entirely transformed musico-cultural ecosystem. (Movement songs have been uploaded on YouTube along with overlapping repertoires from the German Democratic Republic, communist Romania, Yugoslavia, and Bulgaria.) In their heyday, few if anybody had listened to these songs in the privacy of their home. Their compilations on records could hardly be found among the vinyls of music lovers. From the 1990s on, *Best of Communism* afforded its consumers to enjoy (or detest) these songs differently, unburdened from their accrued ideological baggage. Some may even listen to it as music in terms of its efficacy to galvanize a social movement. It enabled older Hungarians to reclaim the songs as a unique capsule storing memories of their younger selves; songs through which the narrative of their personal and communal lives could be pieced together. They became part of vernacular memory mobilizing a range of affect, sentimental or traumatic, amused or bitter, for different participants, depending on their age, background, and their unique place in society as students, workers, party state apparatchiks, or dissidents, prisoners, or draftees. A diverse public thus could learn about, remember, or reassess an era.

Asked by a journalist, a young postal worker admitted that, "I could spend my money in better ways, but if I got it as a present I'd listen to it once in a while, just for fun" (Jordan ibid.). In contrast to this tentative response, an unemployed young man straightforwardly claimed, "That system wasn't good, but better than this one. I owed it to that system and to myself to buy that tape" (Jordan ibid.). Early transition-era euphoria was quickly dispelled by free-market orthodoxy with the dismantling of the safety net inherited from state socialism, all of this costing masses of people their job, a living wage, and often a roof over their head. For them, the hymns and marches directly referred, if not to the utopian future, but to something more palpable: a modest yet solid livelihood. As Maria Todorova aptly observed, "Social memory is selective and contextual. When people evoked the 'good' socialist past, they were not denying the corruption, the shortages, the queues, and the endless intrusions and infringements of the state; rather they were choosing to emphasize other aspects" (2010: 5).

Réthly proposed that it was innocence or naiveté with which masses of people identified with the utopian beliefs propagated by the songs: "Now maybe people can start to face their past, laugh about it, and remember more the good things than the bad" (Jordan ibid.). With this light-hearted statement, he suggested that rather than being victimized, most people had been more or less willing subjects; participants of, rather than resisters to the "socialist experiment." He refrained from attributing guilt or acknowledging the trauma bequeathed by the regime. Instead, he presented a counter narrative to the dour anticommunist political discourse dominating the 1990s, in which both the right and the left had weaponized the "communist past" to compromise prominent personalities on the other side of the aisle. In this regard, his contribution to the nostalgia discourse was similar, as we will see, to "I'll Be Your Plaything."

A series of stage performances, feature films, and video clips also participated in the resurrection of communist movement songs. Renditions ranged from the nostalgic and comic to the surrealistic and hostile parodies. In 2005, the comedic pop singer/actress duo *Pa-dö-dő* (the Hungarian phonetic spelling of the French phrase *pas-de-deux*) starred in a humorous show, performing a medley of pioneer songs where all the "youths" on stage marched to the music clad in Old Navy shirts, drawing in this way a parallel between socialist indoctrination and postsocialist consumerism.[7] The popular cult band, Beatrice, once disfavored by the communist party state for their outspoken oppositional lyrics, came up with an inventive heavy metal/punk hotch-potch of labor movement songs entitled "The Bestest Songs of Our Childhood," [*Gyemekkorunk lexebb dalai*] on a Monty Python-influenced video clip. A more sinister version of this number could be heard on a concert recording where the lead singer, Feró Nagy, who espoused ultra-right politics in the 1990s, introduced the show by yelling menacingly at the audience: "Are there any communists left here"?![8]

2.2. The Dance Song Festival as a Metaphor of János Kádár's Hungary (1956–1988)

Before long the entertainment music of state socialism replaced the movement songs as prime objects of nostalgia. This repertoire, of course, was more complex and more multivocal, allowing the postsocialist public a more nuanced

---

[7]The long-standing duo, formed in 1988 by Mariann Falusi and Györgyi Lang, has been one of the few all-girl groups in Hungarian pop. Their physical appearance boldly disruptive of female beauty standards has been a vital element of their vaudeville-style musical entertainment. The cited song's video recording is available on YouTube "PA-DÖ-DŐ—Koncert 2005" https://www.youtube.com/watch?v=Ycm3jUzc9I4&list=PLG64QfR-KWFL9dC1eQvNXR5-Vda66TyA3&index=55&t=74s (last accessed February 16, 2021).

[8]See "Beatrice—Gyermekkorunk lexebb dalai" https://www.youtube.com/watch?v=CzVlCZ1ZXsQ (last accessed September 5, 2021).

access to private and public memories. At the turn of the 2000s, the Dance Song Festival re-emerged from oblivion. Its new respectability even earned it a tent in Budapest's Sziget Festival, where teens and twentysomethings basked in precisely the kind of conventional, often schmaltzy, schlagers that many of their parents, fans of the 1960s beat movement, loved to hate (Szőnyei 2006). The revival of the Dance Song Festival granted an opportunity for Palya and Gryllus to become musical playmates again. Featuring pop musicians and actors, a stage production by veteran director György Böhm dusted off its winning songs, among them the hit Palya and her mother sang together with such gusto, "I Won't Be Your Plaything." Exceeding expectations, the show "Dance Song Festival! Dance Song Festival?" was so robustly successful that the host theater MÜPA (Palace of the Arts), despite its protocol, re-performed it six months later.

Galvanized by the audience reception and her enjoyment of participating in the show, Palya sought out Gryllus as co-producer and composer to negotiate a record contract with Sony's Hungarian affiliate. They wanted to concoct a cohesive album to capture the interest of the broadest pop audience as well as their peers in folk, world music, and jazz. This was bound to be an unfamiliar adventure. The festival songs registered quite differently even for the two of them. To Palya, the songs were part of her childhood's sonic landscape, the music of her parents' youth, and a cementer of the generations in the family and the larger community. She regarded them as part of the collective auditory unconscious, a form of urban folk music. Taxi drivers, grocery vendors, and hair stylists enjoyed humming along with her whenever she was savoring a number for the album. Bea sought to please all these people and her mother, especially. To Gryllus, in contrast, the same songs had no personal meaning, since his family, like other members of the Hungarian intelligentsia, filtered out commercial pop as a kind of musical junk food. His approach was more detached or ironic. They also admitted that their recent creative adventure with the masterly poetry in *Psyché* only highlighted the aesthetic deficits of the schlager lyrics. Nonetheless, the socialist schlager project tested them in novel ways: How can they dig into their childhood memories and comment on the musical symbols of an era?[9]

If the songs were symbols, the Dance Song Festival lent itself to be treated as an allegory of Kádár-era socialism. The competing songs were churned out by an odd show business constrained by an amalgam of shifting cultural policies and a rigid bureaucracy. Still, the festival was a highly watched spectacle annually broadcast on television between 1966 and 1972. Not only radio and television producers and record industry executives sat on its jury, but leading classical music composers and theatrical directors as well, a residue of the socialist endeavor to eliminate the hierarchy between "high" and "low" culture. The festival even survived the regime change with its last iteration in 1994. Besides representatives of the entertainment industry, the Communist Youth League handed out awards as well. Viewers had a chance to express their tastes by voting. (Early on, households registered their choice of a favorite by turning on all their lights!) The most successful contestants were jolted into solid national stardom. The event had an allure even for high-brow intellectuals such as Ágnes Heller, a philosopher exiled in 1977 for her revisionist Marxist views. This is how she remembered it: "Odd as it may sound

---

[9]Interview with Bea Palya and Samu Gryllus, Budapest, February 13, 2020.

these days, everybody —literally, everybody—watched and listened to the Dance Song Festival. [When it started] not so many households owned a television set, so neighbors also showed up. Everyone rooted for a contestant!" (cited by Murányi and Tóth: 48, trans A.S.).[10]

In what ways did the festival model the regime? How could a popular song contest absorb broader societal conflicts? Pre-rock era popular song production was monopolized by a small number of trained composers, lyricists, and musicians protecting their turf via a range of bureaucratic exclusionary measures, which became defied by an emergent generation of "dissenters," amateur but widely popular beat performers. It was at the festival where masses of middle-aged or older Hungarians were exposed for the first time to rock, soul, and blues re-appropriated in original Hungarian language songs. Despite the initial moral panic, the organizers cautiously ceded room to, while seeking to tame, these newcomers (Kappanyos 2017).

In this regard, the Dance Song Festival mirrored "big politics," more specifically, the Kadarist efforts to incorporate liberal and conservative non-communist voices (mostly of respectable artists, writers, and scientists) into the hegemonic ruling bloc. The regime's relative permissiveness rested on Kádár's gesture of pacifying its critics following the fallen revolution of 1956, by suggesting that: "Whoever is not against us is with us." This was the reversal of his Stalinist predecessor

[10]Some important background data: Hungarian Television started broadcasting in 1957. Even ten years later, it only offered programming on six days of the week, six hours a day on average. Approximately half of the population of ten million owned a television set (Szőnyei, 2006).

Mátyás Rákosi's dictatorial principle treating citizens not strictly aligned with the party-state's doctrines as enemies. Kádár's openness to reconciliation with fellow travelers, on the other hand, was premised on his leverage negotiated with his Soviet overlords trusting him with the task of legitimizing the violently restored communist rule with whatever means he deemed appropriate. This double compromise—with the Soviets and the non-communists—later made it possible for the Communist Party to implement one of the most consequential economic reforms and pluralistic cultural policies within the Soviet Bloc. Hungarians enjoyed a measure of economic well-being, modest yet consistently rising living standards, and freedom in their private pursuits. Yet, in regards to youth culture and popular music, the Kadarist compromise was always circumscribed and subject to withdrawal at any time as the political climate changed (Szemere 2018).

Paradoxically, however, the festival's reconciliation of the older schlager with the young, beat music community implied a balancing game between the Kadarist emphasis on depoliticized leisure and the inevitable *re*-politicization with which beat and rock threatened to reanimate youth culture. Party leaders and top-level media cadres grew nervous that the schlager-oriented world of popular music addressing the conventional themes of boy-meets-girl, courtship, and heartbreak by conforming to a petit-bourgeois moral universe, would be stirred by a different mentality. Along with the immediacy and emotional expressiveness of rock, soul, funk, and beat, a more sincere and less formulaic lyrical language of love relationships emerged. (For example, the song "*Még fáj minden csók*" [Every Kiss Still Hurts] by the band Illés, earning the second prize in 1966, dwelt on the subject's lingering ambivalence in a rekindled romance.)[11] Many of these songs also looked beyond the realm of romance to make social commentary (Lévai and Vitányi 1972). By doing so, beat music rocked the boat of the Kadarist social contract. This tension became particularly palpable after 1968.

Another kind of retro interest in the festival reimagined it more as a Debordian spectacle distracting the public from the regime's fundamentally oppressive nature.[12] The aforementioned show, produced by György Böhm, which spurred Bea to engage with the festival's hits, lured the audience in by promising a nostalgia-infused entertainment with a bite. This is how the Palace of the Arts advertised it:

> …there is no house party where at least one of these schlagers is not played. But there would be little sense in arranging a nostalgia concert that evokes just the 1960s at the Palace of Arts. So we invited performers for these songs to offer a fantastic musical experience to the audience—and *not just to those who like nostalgia.*[13]   [italics by me, A.S.]

Böhm is a member of a generation with personal remembrance of the festivals, in particular, the one held in the summer of

---

[11]Sociological studies such as Bácskai et al. (1969A, 1969B) underlined this feature of beat lyrics to celebrate a fresh new language in pop culture.

[12]Guy Debord, an icon of left radicalism and the art movement Situationism, has authored *The Society of the Spectacle* (1967), where he theorizes modern capitalism as a society in which authentic existence is replaced by appearance and dominated by consumerism.

[13]The event's English language description on MÜPA's program calendar intimates that the show targeted foreign tourists, expats, and émigrés as well. See https://www.mupa.hu/en/program/world-music-jazz-popular-music/dance-song-festival-dance-song-festival-2008-02-22_20-00-bbnh (last accessed March 23, 2021).

1968 when he was a teenager. In our interview he evoked the haunting memory of watching rows of tanks moving northbound on the highway to Czechoslovakia in August that year as part of the concerted Warsaw Pact effort to crack down on its society-wide reform movement associated with Party Secretary Alexander Dubček's leadership and the Prague Spring. Meanwhile, in that same turbulent summer, Böhm was aware, if not part of, the millions of Hungarians staring at their one-channel black-and-white television. People were enthused, enticed, or incensed by the monochrome glitz fest, debating the contestants' appearance, songs, and styles of singing. In his show, Böhm conjured this momentous historical coincidence by constructing "incongruent images" in a campy re-enactment of the song contest.[14] Indeed, we might extend his vision by concluding that, while the military intervention into the Czechoslovakian uprising could not have been subject to public contestation, there was the Dance Song Festival for modernists and conservatives, young and old, social reformers and hardline apparatchiks to clash over the decency of mini skirts, men's long hair, and rock's ecstatic shouts.

---

[14]Personal interview with György Böhm on Skype. July 29, 2020.

3 "Play it One More Time, Play it All Night Long": Recycling, Re-working, and Reflecting in Popular Music Discourse

In Chapter 1 we discussed the ways Palya's and Gryllus's cultural backgrounds and creative talents colluded so serendipitously as to prepare them for the collaborative project of "I'll Be Your Plaything." In Chapter 2 we outlined the wider social and political context in which individual and collective memories of the socialist past became both politicized and marketable. In this chapter we are offering another layer of context to the making of the album by situating it within the global neoliberal culture and the popular music industry, which experienced its own romance with the past known as "retro." Retro as a fashion trend is related to, yet distinct from, postsocialist memorializing. In our overview we will discuss the former's motives, forms, and practices while pointing out, in agreement with George Lipsitz, that the presence of the past in modern popular music "has meaning beyond the lure of nostalgia and the persistence of artistic clichés" (1990: 100). (Although Lipsitz's case study is centered on rock and roll, his claim can be extended to other popular music genres without distorting its meaning.)

3.1. Retroculture, Hauntology, and Necro Marketing

Retro has been Western pop's response to the broader cultural crisis of historical time and collective identity in the aftermath of the Cold War and its East-West divide. Arguably, the "West" suffered its own shock caused by the collapse of existing socialism in Europe. András has pointed out how Western self-image had depended on the existence of its Eastern counterpart.[1] Of particular importance regarding nostalgia and memories is that, with the Soviet Bloc's demise, the paradigm of modernism with its utopian tenets became extinct as well. Whether seen as a threat, a less affluent cousin, or the imperfect yet real alternative to capitalism, the Soviet Bloc had fulfilled the important role of Other for several generations (2008–9: 17–18).

Although the onset of postmodernist retrospection preceded the end of socialism, the latter contributed to a more entrenched sense of "futurelessness." The political scientist Francis Fukuyama famously claimed that the end of history had been attained through the victory of liberal democracy—a prediction almost immediately undermined by the dramatic rise of ethnonationalist conflicts across the post-Soviet region and the Yugoslav wars (see, for example, Ramet 2005). Western cultural critics were particularly concerned that the end of the

---

[1] Andras's essay concerns the Cold War era, but her argument is rooted in Larry Wolff's (1996) seminal study of how Enlightenment philosophers invented Eastern Europe as the backward and barbarian Other of civilized Western Europe.

Cold War left capitalism to be "the only game in town," and with it a state of mind that Mark Fisher (2009) has called "capitalist realism" had arisen. Not coincidentally, the phrase itself is an ironic echo of the term "socialist realism," the mandated aesthetic ideology imposed with varying degrees of success on artists in state socialism. Capitalist realism refers to the widespread resignation among Western progressives to the ubiquity of the marketplace with its deleterious effects on expressive culture, with the drying out of state-sponsored social policies, programs, and the evaporation of even imagined alternatives to the status quo.

In 2011, a book titled *Retromania: Pop Culture's Addiction to Its Own Past* was published by Fisher's fellow critic and friend, Simon Reynolds, observing that "the first ten years of the twenty-first century turned out to be the 'Re' Decade with the dominance of the 're-' prefix: revivals, reissues, remakes, re-enactments. Endless retrospection: every year brought a fresh spate of anniversaries, with their attendant glut of biographies, memoirs, rockumentaries, biopics, and commemorative issues of magazines. Then there were the band reformations, whether it was groups reuniting for nostalgia tours in order to replenish (or to bloat still further) the members' bank balances […] or as a prequel to returning to the studio to relaunch their careers as recording artists" (Location 67).

More worrisome, he goes on, that pop artists have been unable or unwilling to embrace and musically articulate the present time. Even when new music is produced, it does not sound fresh and can be easily mistaken for music created thirtysomething years before. "Once upon a time," Reynolds bemoans, "pop's metabolism buzzed with dynamic energy," but "time itself seemed to become sluggish like a river that starts to meander and form oxbow lakes" (Location 74). To respond to his argument, it's ironic that besides hip hop and EDM, the last innovative and consequential event was punk and postpunk in postwar pop history, sounding the alarm about the lost future and the return of the same. The group Talking Heads formulates this sentiment of "futurelessness" in its ironically wistful song:

The band in heaven
They play my favorite song
Play it one more time
Play it all night long.[2]

After all, it is noted, heaven is boring; nothing ever happens there. Viewed from Reynold's stance, the fading out of pop's present—the past's future—was but the fulfillment of (post) punk's prophecy. In contrast, back in the mid-twentieth century when modernism produced a fast-paced succession of fashionable styles, Adorno observed how soon yesteryear's fashion had lost its appeal and turned alien, provoking widespread derision:

Every moviegoer and every reader of magazine fiction is familiar with the effect of what may be called the obsolete modern: photographs of famous dancers who were alluring twenty years ago, revivals of Valentino films, which though the most glamorous of their day, appear hopelessly old-fashioned … [i]n jazz journalism" any rhythmical formula which is outdated, no matter how "hot" it is in itself, is regarded as ridiculous and therefore either flatly rejected or

2"Heaven" by Talking Heads, of the Album *Fear of Music*. Produced by Talking Heads & Brian Eno, Sire Records, 1979.

enjoyed with the smug feeling that the fashions now familiar
to the listener are superior.

2002: 463

Whether stylistic innovations were genuine or, as Adorno held, merely pseudo-changes, the celebration of the "here and now" in that era stood in stark contrast to the 2000s. Embedded in the cultural condition of postmodernity, retroculture gave dignity to the concept of the old-fashioned and reassessed the value of originality. The capitalist music business and cultural brokers developed an unprecedented appetite for canonization, heritage building, and preservation. Besides institutionalized retrospection, contemporary recording artists have been paying tribute to vintage sounds and idioms via sampling, mashup, and other forms of digital wizardry.

Culture's critical discourse in the 2000s became suffused with metaphors of death. *Hauntology*, Jacques Derrida's pun playing on the French words *hantologie* and *ontologie,* was originally coined to delineate the ghost-like state of Marxism after the end of the Cold War. This is how Peter Buse and Andrew Stott interpret the concept:

> Ghosts arrive from the past and appear in the present. However, the ghost cannot be properly said to belong to the past. Does then the "historical" person who is identified with the ghost properly belong to the present? Surely not, as the idea of a return from death fractures all traditional conceptions of temporality. The temporality to which the ghost is subject is therefore paradoxical, at once they "return" and make their apparitional debut.
>
> cited by Fisher 2013: 44

Hauntology became an umbrella term not only for the bustling academic field of memory and nostalgia studies, but for the fine art world's preoccupation with archives, ruins, traces, and family histories.[3] Reynolds and Fisher adopted the term to characterize intriguing trends in experimental rock and electronic music whose practitioners had "scavenged" indie record shops and digital libraries for the most arcane recordings, such as early sci-fi film and television music, (British) Public Service announcements, and muzak, in search of traces of their childhood. The object of nostalgia in these artefacts is not the time period *per se*—from, say, the 1950s to the 1980s— as Reynolds explains, but a zeitgeist characterized by feeling truly home in the present and exhilarated about the future. Yet it is also clear from his critical narrative that as retro fashion cycles continue to shrink and the sought-after past increasingly means the past decade, the affective states conveyed via the recycled music would no longer offer escapes to an era when time was *not* perceived as out-of-joint. To extend this line of reasoning, the likes of the Sex Pistols, the Dead Kennedys, or the Talking Heads are a case in point in representing the historical moment—the "here and now"—while voicing a sense of fractured temporality and alienation.

Thus the questions follow: Was punk the harbinger of the hauntological era of pop? Or was it pop history's last moment sans nostalgia? The two statements may not be mutually exclusive. Music critics identify the 1980s as the beginning of the "Re" era with its infatuation with the 1950s, but the decade has

---

[3]A noteworthy example is the Hungarian filmmaker and media artist Péter Forgács's internationally acclaimed work—films and installations— re-contextualizing old family home movies (1920s to 1960s) to capture the intersection of twentieth-century history and ordinary people's personal lives.

also been remembered affectionately as a vibrant time period that bred new wave, postpunk, world music, and hip hop.[4]

The sociologist Jean Hogarty (2016) looked at the retro phenomenon from the consumers' end, to find that young fans shared a *hauntological* structure of feeling marked by their unfamiliarity with, or disinterest in, contemporary pop and rock.[5] They also frequently shared their parents' musical taste, deeming their choices more authentic than current styles fed to them by the mass media. Their nostalgia was vicarious, expressed in a longing for an era they had never experienced personally.

Another spectral metaphor in contemporary popular music is necro marketing, allegedly one of the most dynamic branches of the twenty-first century media industry. A remarkable example is Tupac Shakur engaging with his former friend-turned-enemy The Notorious B.I.G. in posthumous dialogue on the rap number "Runnin' [Dying to Live]," years after their deaths. Tupac's other posthumous releases have sold equally well (Stanyek and Piekut 2010). The highlight of the Coachella Festival of 2012 was Tupac's hologram-like

[4]For example, a bustling musical underground subculture existed in Hungary during the 1980s that had largely vanished by the 1990s, partly because of the tumultuous political changes that overshadowed it. Interviews with musicians and fans, as well as the bands' repeated reunions and realignments producing relatively little new output, revealed the prevalence of sustained reflective nostalgia for the1980s (Szemere 2010: 253–6), a sentiment aptly captured in the title of a recently published poster collection: *Pokoli aranykor* (Infernal Golden Age) *New wave plakátok a 80-as évekből*. Bp Szabó György és Szőnyei Tamás gyűjteményeiből. (New Wave posters from the 1980s. A Selection of György Bp. Szabó and Tamás Szőnyei's collections.) Budapest, Hungary 2017.
[5]A "structure of feeling" is a concept developed by the literary and cultural theorist Raymond Williams, a founder of British Cultural Studies. It refers to distinctive yet widespread patterns of organizing experience in art and cultural practices of a particular historical period. Typically, structures of feeling are in tension with the official ideology of a society.

revivification on stage—next to the real-life presence of Snoop Dogg—addressing an audience he had never seen with words he had never actually spoken. Posthumous releases and novel musical concoctions, including dead celebrities' tracks, have become so lucrative that for many artists, Steve Jones (2005) believes, the best career move is to die.

Finally, we must address the most conspicuous facet of retro culture, the proliferation of covers. The industry has been widely criticized for the numerous excuses to release old music in new renditions (Plasketes 2005, Padget 2020). Tribute albums occasioned by a celebrity musician's birthday have been complemented with tribute collections honoring the anniversary of an album's release; the word-by-word replay of a cult band's concert by a tribute band no longer raises eyebrows. In 2001, Grammy established an award for the best Traditional Pop Vocal album, even though, as George Plasketes pointed out, the meaning of "traditional," originally referring to the pre-rock era, was soon broadened to include the repertoire of major artists in rock, blues, and folk, such as David Bowie, Joni Mitchell, or The Cure (143). The commercial motive and risk aversion behind recent practices of re-recording pop are tied up with the structure and workings of media monopolies incentivized in cross-promoting a range of products. Movies popularize cover versions of vintage songs, which in turn sell the movies, along with soundtrack albums, video games, and merchandise—think of the highly effective reuse of Leonard Cohen's song "Hallelujah" (1984) and the Monkees' hit "I'm a Believer" (1967) in Dreamworks' 2001 animated family movie Shrek.[6]

---

[6]"Hallelujah" was re-invented by Rufus Wainwright on Shrek's soundtrack album, but because of royalty/label conflicts, John Cale's rendition appeared on the movie. The songwriter of "I'm a Believer" was Neil Diamond, performed by *Smash Mouth*.

Covering is also motivated by the pressure exerted on musicians to keep their names in the news by releasing albums every few years. The singing talent shows, a hugely successful reality television format globally franchised under various names, such as Pop Idol, The X Factor, [X country's] Got Talent, etc. in the 2000s further popularized the practice of re-performing copyrighted songs. The excessive reliance on covering along with other symptoms of slumping innovation has raised questions about musicians' lack of sufficient creative time, especially among newcomers and marginalized social groups (withdrawal from day jobs and from superficial Internet-based sociality in order to produce art), as well as material resources under the constraints of neoliberal capitalism to experiment with and develop their musical ideas without the support and convenience of music's familiarity with the public (Fisher 2014: 331–44; Reynolds 2011; Lange 2018: 189–91).

3.2. The Critique of the Hauntological Reason

The hauntological critique of retromania, while offering incisive points, tends to conflate two problems. One concerns the aesthetic deficits of new popular music for lacking innovation, sounding unremarkable, or, in Fisher's succinct formulation, "performing anachronism."[7] The other problem focuses on certain musical artists' creative engagement with various vintage

---

[7]Fisher's (2014) examples of anachronism include The Arctic Monkeys' 2005 single "I Bet You Look Good on the Dancefloor," Amy Winehouse's version of "Valerie," and Adele's songs. Fisher here extends Frederic Jameson's concept of "nostalgia mode," 250–65; 313–18.

sounds and styles perceived as "futuristic," that is, displaying thrill about the future as a supersession of the present. The former critique implies a negative aesthetic judgment about a musical piece, style, or performance, the likes of which dominate much of the media. The latter is an argument about the so-called hauntological structure of feeling, a kind of melancholy sensibility which, in consciously escaping to the past, indirectly comments on the present. The concept of nostalgia is central to both phenomena. When a song is played on a city's number one pop hits radio station, although sounding like it could easily be aired on the 1980s station, we have the impression that past and present have collapsed, time has stopped moving forward. This kind of music can be regarded as parasitically nostalgic for not signaling distance from what it feeds on. In contrast, the creative practice of "hauntological" musicians could aptly be described by Boym's notion of reflective nostalgia. Reflective nostalgiacs tend to be ironists aware of having no straight paths back to the past; or, to quote Bob Dylan, having "no direction home." This awareness does not prevent them from being fascinated with the ambivalences of yearning and remembering. Reflective nostalgia is highly aesthetically productive. It can also produce communities and subcultures. Some of the most captivating and memorable songs and performances of the Hungarian underground rock of the 1980s narrate passionate or wistful escapes from the present to an indistinct "elsewhere" in time and space, yet the object of yearning, once envisioned, turns out to disappoint (Szemere 2010: 249–53). The form of nostalgia Boym has less respect for is known as *restorative*, and is premised on the plausibility of an easy return to some idealized past by reviving or rather reinventing its traditions, in the sense Eric Hobsbawm (1983) has observed. Ethnonationalist and fundamentalist religious movements tend to feed on restorative nostalgia. The national rock scene in Hungary exemplifies this mindset with its ultra-right conservatism and grief over Hungary's territorial loss in the wake of World War One (Feischmidt and Pulay 2017).

Reflection and irony, however, are no longer exclusive to musicians with progressive, liberal, or anticapitalist affiliation, as attested to by the American Alt-right's and other extremist movements' re-appropriation of vaporwave, an electronic music trend closely related to hauntology. Fashwave and Trumpwave, *qua* music can barely be distinguished from vaporwave, since they all deal with the "eviscerated junkspace of the postmodern age" (Cole 2020) and claim as their forerunners such 1980s iconic bands as Joy Division and Depeche Mode, even though the latter protested against the attribution of ancestry (Bullock and Kerry 2017). Yet the fascistic underbelly of a formerly ideologically elusive movement is increasingly evident. Most examples of Fashwave and Trumpwave on YouTube—those that have not yet been removed by Google—combine the vintage sounds with harshly propagandistic images and soundbites from political speeches in a manner that undercuts any semblance of irony or double entendre.

3.2.1. Dialogism and the realm of the intermundane

Reynolds's critique of retro culture, we have argued, collapsed the hauntological structure of feeling with commercial strategies. Yet it is useful to look at approaches in popular music studies that treat the incorporation of past styles, traditions, and sounds as neither nostalgic nor cynically business oriented, but rather as a normal modus operandi in creating new works. Musical dialogism is one of them.

Dialogism was originally developed by the Russian literary theorist Mikhail Bakhtin to interpret the ways the modern novel incorporates "voices," that is, sociologically specific uses of language in dialogue or polyphony with one another. In music, various melodic and rhythmic motifs, instrumental arrangements, vocal techniques, musical quotations, and samples may represent these "voices" with which contemporary musicians enter into conversation. Applied to early rock and roll, Lipsitz has demonstrated the presence of the African American past in such formal features as the blues structure, falsettos, and call-and-response, which he traced back to West-African music and poetry. But one may counter, don't music historians routinely trace specific musical forms and expressive devices back to their earlier iterations when asking questions such as "What has Beethoven done to the scherzo form"? or "How does bebop retain the feel of swing"? Dialogism does the tracing also, but accentuates historicity differently. First, the emphasis is not on the attained formal unity of a piece incorporating historical elements, but on its (relative) multivocality. Second, dialogism highlights the politics of borrowing from and referencing past traditions. In hip hop, for example, the politics of sampling and quoting more often than not express a musician's artistic and cultural indebtedness to predecessors in a range of genres such as jazz, funk, gospel, and blues. Dialogues conceived in this sense can also musically articulate identity politics.

Another alternative approach to music's interaction with the past is proposed by Jason Stanyek and Benjamin Piekut's seminal study (2010), which dwells on pop's retrospection, not as a business practice or a structure of feeling, but as a problem of productive agency. Questioning established notions of authorship and artistic agency, Stanyek and Piekut believe that the difference between living and dead contributors in the production process is overstated. Conventionally, live musical actors are seen to possess all the creative agency in terms of determining what and how musical and technological resources—instruments, recordings, computer hardware, and software—should be employed to produce their work. Conversely, agency is not attributed to dead musicians participating in the production process through their existing soundtracks only; the latter are treated as inanimate resources.

Drawing on the intricate—and at times unpredictable— microprocesses taking place in the recording studio, Stanyek and Piekut revise the idea of creative agency to suggest that it is being *distributed* rather than being the sole property of living individual artists. Inspired by Bruno Latour's sociological use of actor-network theory (ANT), they look at an artefact's *effectivity* made possible by human and non-human, as well as live and dead "actors" of a network.[8] The implications of this approach for retroculture lie in refocusing our attention to the complex and productive *collaborations* between past and present musical works, sound recordings, technologies, and discourses, as well as between live and dead humans.

The site of this collaboration is the realm of what Stanyek and Piekut call the *intermundane,* defined as "the arrangements of interpenetration between worlds of living and dead" (14). From such an angle, digital technologies deployed to recycle and recombine old(er) music are not parasitic on the past or enfeebling the present. Neither are they the readily available

---

[8]The sociological application of ANT aims to break down the abstract notion of the "social" (used in stock phrases such as "social forces" and "social structure") by closely examining the shifting networks of relationships between objects, discourses, processes, technologies, and human beings on the ground.

tools of endless repetition and retrospection. Instead, these technologies are active participants ("actors") in making a difference; they enable the re-articulation of old and new sound materials, often in uncanny ways.

The larger arguments involved in both musical dialogism and the distribution of creative agency via the intermundane, apply to the practice of covering a song written or first recorded by someone else. Covering initiates a dialogic relationship with music and musicians of earlier times (although contemporary musicians often cover each other's music as well), where a certain set of parameters in the cover version is identical with those in the covered musical piece (for example, the melody, the lyrics, or the chord sequence, etc.). This dialogue may be overt or covert, depending on the listener, who may or may not be aware of hearing an "original" or a cover version. The concept of the intermundane applies to covering less in a technical and literal sense than a metaphoric sense, and only to cases where the original producers of the song are no longer alive. Even in this restricted sense, though, the notion of the intermundane means bridging the past with the present, connecting musicians of different eras, places, and even zeitgeists via the interpretation of a song.

Covering, like musical quotation, DJing and sampling, is but another form of intertextuality in popular music. The practice is common, yet the *term* itself is not known in jazz where the re-performance of a well-known musical piece called a jazz standard serves as a source text for performers to display their improvisatory skills and unique take on a composition. Neither does the term make sense in classical music where, in contrast to jazz, the score retains its primary importance, yet no status distinction is made between the score's first and hundredth performance. A score exists for a potentially endless number of renditions. Finally, the concept is unknown in traditional (premodern) music cultures where the authorship and ownership of music is unmarked. In contrast, modern commercial popular music, centered on the recorded sound, legal, and business arrangements (copyright, royalty, performing rights) remunerate the producers of the original version. If, on the other hand, a more recent rendition (the "cover") gains more popularity, the new performers become "owners" of the song in the public's mind.[9]

With the onset of the rock era in the 1960s, writing and performing one's own music became the norm, and was thus bound up with rock's key aesthetic and political value, authenticity. But, paradoxically, with the heritagization of rock, authenticity has become a contested term, with popular musicians feeling less constrained by the demand of performing their own songs only. An example is Bryan Ferry venting his frustration: "Covers—I hate that term. To me a cover is just changing the vocal performance. I like to redesign a song. That's really a modern idea, after Dylan [...] that you have to write your own stuff. The idea that you can write your whole repertoire yourself seems rather conceited" (DeCurtis 1993, 20). In a similar vein, Emmylou Harris asserted that "Songs need new voices to sing them in places they've never been sung in order to stay alive" (quoted in Plasketes, ibid. 138). And analogously to jazz, some pop and rock songs—most notably, McCartney's "Yesterday," Lennon's "Imagine," the Rolling Stones' "I Can't Get No Satisfaction," each known to be re-recorded by thousands of performers—do function as "standards"

---

[9]Whitney Houston's re-recording of the hit "I Will Always Love You" ended up so popular—largely because of being featured in the 1992 Hollywood movie *The Bodyguard* starring Houston—that most listeners associate the song with her rather than its composer and first performer in 1974, Dolly Parton.

(Keightley 2017). The question is whether pop and rock would entirely follow jazz's trajectory by decoupling composition from performance as the basis of authenticity and originality, or the band/songwriting or singer/songwriter formula remains privileged.

In conclusion, musical dialogism and, in a restricted sense, the concept of the intermundane, allow us to reframe the problem of retrospection and retro culture. Instead of simply seeing it as contemporary musicians' absence of inspiration, nostalgic escape, or cashing in on another artist's hits, retrospection, in many instances, can be meaningful, politically charged, innovative, and, in a sense, an inevitable engagement with specific styles, voices, and genres of past musics. The meaning and value of the new music thus produced depends on what is borrowed, with what intent, how the borrowed elements are incorporated, and to what effects. This will be the concern of our next chapter.

4 Start Making a New Sense

Having guided our readers through the musical articulations of nostalgia, postsocialist memorializing, hauntology, and retro culture, it may be evident by now that the making of the album "I'll Be Your Plaything" was inspired by complex feelings about history, culture, and popular music. In this chapter we will dwell on the question, how can a set of reconceived old pop songs and schlagers tell a story? Primarily, of course, through the historical dialogue with the songs selected and the manner of their covering, a process into which Bea and Samu will offer us some glimpses. Later in the chapter we will suggest a typology of covers bridging international examples with the album's songs and taking a closer look at both the originals and their re-inventions on "I'll Be Your Plaything."

Before proceeding to that, a few words about the album's design. Some covers are meaningfully connected with preludes and interludes as well as with "traces" in the sense Walter Benjamin has construed the term, believing that carefully selected images, quotes, and facts are traces of social relations, and their presentation and interpretation captures the character of an era.[1] Two such traces are recorded on our album, one from

---

[1] The grandiose, yet unfinished, work associated with Benjamin's historiographic method is *The Arcades Project*. Ed. R. Tiedemann. Trans. H. Eiland and K. McLaughlin. Cambridge, MA: Harvard University Press, 1999.

the 1960s and a contemporary one—a kind of "aural snapshot"—created by the producers in the studio. In this sense, "I'll Be Your Plaything" is a unique "hauntological" concept album whose narrative is stitched together from diverse musical numbers and fragments from the past and present. Let us see how.

4.1. Traces of the Past and the Present

The older trace on the album is an amateur tape recording prepared at the garment factory of Szeged (a mid-size city in Southern Hungary) where Bea's mother worked in 1969, and it is a key aural "actor" of the album. On it, Emike Sztáncs, Bea's mother, and her co-workers were getting ready to celebrate the name day of another brigade member, a common workplace ritual usually held at the end of a shift.[2] The tape became a family heirloom, which Bea had listened to dozens of times while growing up. Recycled and fragmented on a cover album such as I'll Be Your Plaything, it serves as a humorous or, at times, grotesque trace of everyday life at a socialist workplace. Samu and his sound engineers spread the segments across the length of the album in a way skits are inserted between songs on hip hop albums. The protagonist—or rather emcee—of the celebration was the boss, Comrade Kozocsa, who, in a manner both patronizing and cheesy, encouraged his all-female brigade to record a song for the celebrant. The more he presses them to sing, the more they

---

[2]The celebration of one's given name is originally a Christian tradition associated with Roman Catholicism and Eastern Orthodoxy.

resist, spurring him to become arrogant. The listener can hear the women's embarrassed giggling in the background. The awkwardness of the scene reminded us of the annual workplace rituals of commemorating International Women's Day on March 8 in socialist-era Hungary. All across the country—from ministries to police precincts, from schools to factories, and from department stores to research institutes, the management—the director, the local communist party secretary, and the trade union's representative—convened the employees to greet women with clichés of accolades and a tiny bouquet of flowers, praising them for their "triple shifts" as employees, mothers, and housewives.

The album's other trace is an aural meditation on copyrights and authorship occasioned by improvising on American musical pieces. Recorded on the multi-track piece "America" (*Amerika*), the listeners can "peek" into the backstage of the production process. Starting with a tribute to the American composer, John Philip Sousa, Gryllus's instrumental piece for brass (track #23) appears as an ironic reference to the United States as a military superpower. Subsequently, a transatlantic conversation is heard between Bea and Samu on Skype about the copyright restrictions of the music cited on some version of the ongoing track, which was supposed to be removed. Meanwhile, the band members are goofing around on the cello, the tuba, and various percussives, improvising cacophonously on Leonard Bernstein's *West Side Story*, Stephen Foster's nineteenth-century song "Oh! Suzanna" (whose Hungarian language variant is known as children's folklore), Bruce Springsteen tunes, and more. The listener wonders whether *these* were the fragments that had to be cleared? Or are we hearing a "mutilated" version of "America"? A third layer is added to the musical chaos with the cover of an old

Hungarian schlager titled "America," back from the 1930s (composed by operettists Alfréd Márkus and Ferenc Martos[3]) sardonically eulogizing America as "a gigantic country," a "thousand-story heaven," which it must have seemed in the eyes of millions of East-European migrants seeking relief from poverty or persecution there. Some eighty years later, the mocking tone of the song resonated with these young Hungarians whose unruly play on the tracks reveals a complex mix of awe, desire, fantasy, and frustration with the world's most mythicized country—and a superpower of music.

Samu's account of the legal tangles prompts Bea to ask what may be one of the album's central philosophical—and also legal—questions: "Then who wrote this all"? Instead of answering, Samu is encouraging Bea to rap this question to the rhythm of the underlying rudimentary hip hop beat (presumably recorded earlier than the conversation). Thus the question becomes rhetorical and is left hanging in the air: Who defines musical authorship and ownership and on what grounds? How arbitrary can such definitions be to even make sense? How do transnational legal terms (adaptation,

---

[3]During the first four decades of the twentieth century, the United States was more of an importer of popular music than an exporter, and Central European musical theater was highly sought after on Broadway. Ferenc Martos gained renown as a Hungarian librettist and a translator of several operettas, such as *The Marriage Market* and *Sybill* by Victor Jacobi and *Alexandra* by Alfréd Szirmai, which came to be adapted to the stages of London and New York, as revealed by the monograph *The German Operetta on Broadway and in the West End*,1900–1940 by Derek B. Scott (Cambridge University Press, 2019). Scott's title is misleading, though, since most of these artists—including such classics as Franz Lehar and Imre Kálmán—were not German but multilingual citizens of the Austro-Hungarian Monarchy (until its demise in 1918), whose plays premiered in Berlin before their transfer to the metropolises of the United Kingdom and the United States.

arrangement, and traditional music) work in an improvisatory meditation on "America" pieced together from a random collection of Broadway tunes, minstrel songs, classical, and rock hits?

4.2. The Creative Process

With a genuinely hauntological mindset, Samu set out with a big duffel bag to Budapest's famed music store with a large catalog called *Rózsavölgyi*, and returned with dozens of entertainment music scores, most of them having premiered at the Dance Song Festival, although, as we have seen, a few dated back to the early twentieth century. This is how Bea depicts the onset of their creative work:

> We took notes on index cards, browsing through YouTube channels, sitting over one or another song for half a day humming the tunes and beating the rhythms, and trying out sonorities. We sought out particular [musical] moods, talking them over a bit, and recording strips of music until we got stuck and then returned to the drawing board.
>
> Palya 2011, 240

As opposed to their elation—and anxiety—in working with Sándor Weöres' lyrics, Bea initially felt distanced from the schlagers, so "we worked hard to remold them into our own" (ibid. 238). But a workplace is sometimes just a hair breadth away from the playground. Since the songs had been woven into the fabric of their youth (especially Bea's), they looked both for the material and aural traces of those years. They were digging through the Chinese market of Budapest and returned with a bulk of cheap musical toys, such as a plastic guitar suited to sound a major scale, a kitschy music box, a pretty flute with pink keywork, and a rolling doll (*kelj-fel baba*) singing out of tune. All these toys received a role in the instrumentation and appeared on the CD's enclosed folded leaflet alongside other requisites of a typical young Hungarian girl's bedroom at the turn of the 1980s (see Figure 5 on p. 78). Once surrounded by these props, "the musical raw material invited us to play … Like kids with their new toy, we disassembled and reassembled, turned and twisted them" (ibid. 241).

What makes music sound hauntological beyond evoking old tunes? A favored practice of referencing obsoleteness and historically shifting encounters with music is to incorporate the sounds of old musical technology. In the 1970s and 1980s, Hungarians had the opportunity to purchase many different kinds of music on vinyl, but they could tape a broader variety of genres and styles from local and foreign (read: Western) radio stations. "We remembered," Bea writes in her memoir, "how we collected music from radio so that occasionally we could push the rec button with a delay, in the middle of the song's first verse or, by chance, recorded the programmer's last words of intro as well. And do you remember hearing this screeching high-pitched sound of the recorder twisting the tape when pushing the rec button just half-way? … On the album we employed these sound effects …" (ibid. 240). Indeed, the listener can detect the hissing of the record player's needle on the grooves at the end of track #32 ("Time Stands Still" [*Megáll az idő*]), and similar sounds are audible on the spliced-in fragments of the old tape recording of the name day celebration.

4.3. Deconstruction and Dialogues

Commenting on the album, the critic Zsolt Podhorányi (2010) observed: "An original musical piece covered by a supreme musician can alter it entirely or accentuate it so differently that we wonder whether lyrics and melody are indeed the core components of a schlager"? (11. trans. A.S). Implied in this comment are two points. First, the form of a *schlager* affords a certain kind of attention and mode of listening in that melody and lyrics enjoy pride of place over, say, instrumentation, chord progression, or vocal delivery. (With the immense impact of African-American idioms and sophistication of music production technologies throughout the twentieth century, however, features like rhythm, vocal timbre, riffs, or dynamics have become quite salient as well.) Many believe that a schlager's success depends on the melody's hummability. The journalist Matthew Parris remarked that "'superior' musicians who ignore such a simple ingredient are the parasites on a beast whose lifeblood is melody" (cited by Phillips 2006). Most songs selected on Bea's album belong to this class of hummable and whistle-able popular songs.

The second point following from Podhorányi's remark is that, by making the listener conscious of the multiple features a piece of music is molded of, Bea and Samu have deconstructed the schlager, subjecting it to compositional and performance techniques through which the familiar reappear as oddly unfamiliar. But un-familiarization was but one method to erode the dominant status of melody and lyrics. By shifting the tempos, giving a new instrumental or rhythmic treatment, reconceiving the song's structure, or crossing genre boundaries across and within a musical track, the album as a whole traverses a range of emotional registers from melancholic ("The Big Voyage," "Life Goes On," "The Rain and Me") to defiant ("I Won't Be Your Plaything," "I Don't Wanna Get Married by All Means"), from contemplative ("Trees, Flowers, Light," "Time Stands Still") to ecstatic ("After me, the Deluge," "Invocatio"), and from ironic ("Baby," "America") to jaunty ("Part-Time Lover," "You Can't Fall Asleep Next to Me") to poignant ("The Ballad of Blond Annie"). The variety of moods and sentiments does not result in some nostalgic hotch-potch. Instead, the album cleverly intertwines the serious with the comedic, and reflection on personal and collective pasts is coupled with a keen sense of living in the present. The most intriguing features of such a concept album derive from intricate parallels and contrasts between "now" and "then," "here" and "elsewhere," or "us" and "them," referring to generational, ethnic, and gender identities. A geographical dimension is added to the historical via the diverse musical styles and traditions conjured. As listeners, we are presented with a curious, at times dizzying, conversation between sounds and voices of old village life and modern global cityscapes, persons and personas of present and distant social worlds.

4.4. Uncovering: Types of Cover Songs

Since the practice of covering has grown from a trend into a subgenre in the retro era, attempts have been made to take stock of its various modalities (Plasketes 2005, Mosser 2008). Highlighting the commercial aspects of producing covers, in the previous chapter we argued that whereas covering is a taken-for-granted practice across traditions and genres—from folk to classical music and from jazz to pop and rock—the term is only relevant in commercial popular music where the distinction between composer and performer carries legal, commercial, cultural, and political ramifications. In this section we will delve into the non-commercial strategies of covering popular music, albeit with the caveat that commercial, political, and aesthetic considerations can at times be hopelessly entangled. The appropriation of black rhythm and blues in the early 1950s by white America is a case in point. Initially disfavored by major record companies and radio stations, the music became more palatable for mass consumption via white performers' versions (Gillett 1983, Keightley 2003). In this practice the aesthetic motive of "bleaching" the music to cater to a wider public cannot meaningfully be sorted out from white recording artists' and the majors' intent to materially benefit from marginalizing African-American competitors.

Covers may be classified in numerous ways, although as Mosser points out, they are fraught with difficulties and ambiguities. What should we call, for instance, a version interpreted by its author after a performer has turned it into a hit? The boundaries can also be blurry between various types. A useful organizing principle is the covering artist's intent, even though intents can be multiple. Besides paying tribute to a songwriter-performer, a song, or an album, an interpreter may also wish to crystallize their musical persona or demonstrate their mastery of the musical idiom that the original piece represents. Mosser furthermore wonders how in some situations even one of the covering artist's intentions can be figured. We may add that, given music's polysemic nature—its susceptibility to multiple valid interpretations—

does the musicians' intent matter so much as to override alternative readings by the audience? In the case of ironic covers, for example, the difference between encoded and decoded meanings can elicit debates among fans, critics, and the general public. The Slovenian countercultural group Laibach presents one of the most theorized cases of elusive meanings and multiple (mis)interpretations (Mendelyté 2019, Spaskovska 2011). Reviled by the socialist Slovenian (Yugoslav) media for supporting fascism with their assemblage of totalitarian symbols, most fans enjoyed Laibach's spectacles as ironic. Slavoj Žižek (2012), for one, impugned this perception, arguing that ambiguity and duplicity is endemic to oppressive regimes—whether socialist or capitalist—and Laibach merely holds a mirror to the operation of power in late modern society.[4]

*　　*　　*

With Mosser's warnings in mind, we set up a typology pertaining to the musical commentary Bea and Samu have made on their memories and perceptions of Hungary's past on the album "I'll Be Your Plaything." Before moving on to the song descriptions, we will establish the viability of such a classification by reference to a few international and Hungarian musical examples.

Paying homage. Regarding covers, many music fans will likely think of the most habitual gesture in the music business, expressing reverence to the greats of a genre—the likes of Joni Mitchell, Bob Dylan, James Brown, or The Beatles. Tributes are

---

[4]Slavoj Žižek—¿De qué se trata Laibach? https://www.youtube.com/watch?v=1EoNvGWAgjw&t=80s (last accessed November 19, 2020).

paid to important albums as well. The recent re-recording of the Talking Heads' *Remain in Light* (1980) by the Beninese singer Angelique Kidjo, for example, threw light on the fascinating and complex aesthetic adventure of (re-)appropriations between white Western and black African musicians (Grow 2018). A subcultural style linked with a place and time has inspired a new generation of Hungarian punk and hardcore bands (Piss Crystals, Norms, and others), as testified to by the Hungarian album *Egy dicső nemzet kifordult gyomra* (The Upset Stomach of a Glorious Nation), to revivify the best of their 1980s precursors such as Marina Revue, Trottel, and the Galloping Coroners (Dömötör 2018). Lastly, musical memorializing involves tribute bands' or impersonators' acts of replicating a star performer's entire musical output. The Hungarian Syrius Tribute Band, besides replaying the 1970s legendary jazz-rock outfit's numbers, also takes care of its heritage.

Crystallizing a recording artist's individuality, persona, and performance style represents another goal of appropriation entailing various degrees of interventions. The interpretation may be considered minor if the integrity of the song (tempo, melody, lyrics, instrumentation) is preserved (Mosser ibid) as in Lady Gaga's faithful rendition of Edith Piaf's "La Vie en Rose." At the other end of the spectrum, a major interpretation alters one or more musical features drastically enough to impress the listener as hearing a virtually different song. Tom Waits's raspy, faltering voice and slurry diction—his grain of voice—in the song "Somewhere" from *West Side Story,* deviates so far from the conventional Broadway-style of singing that a whole new meaning—one of shattered dreams and utter desperation—arises from it.

Interpretations may "walk the line" between genre boundaries, as heard on Johnny Cash's *American Recordings.*

Pop/rock songs by The Beatles, Nine Inch Nails, and Depeche Mode have metamorphosed via Cash's unique take on them into blends of outlaw country, folk song, and chanson. It is not uncommon that the covering artist becomes the new "owner" of a song via a re-recording that outshines the original. Aretha Franklin's celebrated rendition of Otis Redding's "Respect" and its consecration as a feminist anthem had Redding acknowledge her ownership with an affectionate laugh: "This is a song that a girl took away from me, a good friend of mine" (cited by Freeman 2001).[5]

Localization refers to the ubiquitous practice of imbuing an international hit typically produced in the center of the global music business with the musical, lyrical, or performance characteristics of a (sub)culture in a specific regional, national, or genre context. How was a romantic American song, for instance, localized by small addition to its lyrics so as to morph into the chronicler of collective trauma in Kadarist Hungary? The song "Que Sera, Sera" (Jay Livingston and Ray Evans) made famous by Doris Day in Alfred Hitchcock's 1956 film *The Man Who Knew Too Much*, received the Academy Award of Best Original Song, became a chart topper in the US and Britain, and before long was performed in more than a dozen languages, including Hungarian. On October 23 of the same year, Hungarians launched a revolution to topple their Stalinist rulers, which was crushed by Soviet tanks eighteen days later.

During this time period the borders with Austria were open, prompting 200,000 citizens of the country to flee. The Hungarian lyrics of "Que Sera' (translated as "Ahogy lesz, úgy

[5]Scott Freeman is quoted in Malawey (2014: 186).

lesz" by György G. Dénes) memorializes this exodus in an added verse about the singer-protagonist's boyfriend, who left her "and is far away now," keeping her in doubt about his ever returning. (Considered *defectors* until their rehabilitation a decade later, the illegal emigrants of the revolution could not visit back for more than a decade; their letters were monitored or lost.) "Que Sera" conveyed for Hungarians more than the sorrow over the unpredictability of love affairs, as Doris Day's version did; the song absorbed the societal grief over the defeated uprising followed by the displacements and separation of loved ones. Even though the cover version's reference to the mass defection was oblique, the restored communist regime's bureaucrats blacklisted the song, which has nonetheless remained alive in public memory and been re-recorded by a number of singers.[6]

Ironic and humorous covers. Intimately related to playing in and with music, irony and humor are a ubiquitous feature of popular music. Similarly to the generation of caricatures, memes, and jokes of all forms, humorous covers of pop hits are perpetually produced in our late modern entertainment-spewing media culture.

Frequently, a song is parodied with new lyrics in order to address a current issue. A recent example is Chris Mann's cover

---

[6]MTI, "Elhunyt az 'Ahogy lesz, úgy lesz' szerzője" *hvg.hu*, February 18, 2007. https://hvg.hu/kultura/20070218_rayevans (last accessed November 1, 2020). For the best-known versions of the song on YouTube, see "Hollós Ilona—Ahogy lesz úgy lesz" https://www.youtube.com/watch?v=pHKONQ5frBk&feature=emb_rel_pause and Koncz Zsuzsa—Ahogy lesz, úgy lesz https://www.youtube.com/watch?v=J3WSIM0OrJ4 (last accessed November 1, 2020).

version of Adele's "Hello" on the individual's tribulations of quarantined life during the coronavirus pandemic.[7]

4.5. Translations and Radical Hybrids: Cover Songs on "I'll Be Your Plaything"

Paying homage? Although the album contains no express statements of reverence regarding any particular musical style, piece, or performer, the singer Kati Kovács is featured by three tracks: "I Won't Be Your Plaything" (#2), "Oh Lord, Give Us Some Rain" (#28), and "The Rain and Me" (#29). In light of Bea's intimacy with non-white and non-Western musical traditions, her fascination with Kati's soul-flavored, sultry voice is no surprise. Critics and audiences have admired the two singers for a similar set of qualities, such as their distinctive vocal tone, emotional energy, and expressiveness, as well as their ease of movement between styles and idioms. Kati and Bea have both garnered praise for their free-spirited assertive personality and control over their career in a heavily masculinist music business, an issue to be revisited in Chapter 5.[8]

The song "Oh Lord, Give Us Some Rain" (track #28), was unique in its time with Kati's soul singing over a hard rock arrangement (composed by Tibor Koncz and Iván Szenes). No

---

[7]Fernandez, Celia. A man's parody of Adele's "Hello" about being stuck inside is the relatable quarantine humor we all need. *Insider* Apr 2, 2020 https://www.insider.com/hello-from-the-inside-adele-parody-chris-mann-2020-4.
[8]See the journalist András Szegő's accolade on Kati Kovács's official website https://www.kovacskati.hu/index.html (last accessed November 6, 2020). Regarding Bea, see Völgyi (2014).

less of an outlier was the song's theme among the contestants of the Dance Song Festival of 1972, a spiritual yearning for rain. The lyricist even worried that the inclusion of "God" in the title might disqualify the song.[9] Instead it won first prize, followed by a trophy in Dresden, the German Democratic Republic. (The somewhat haphazard workings of censorship were a salient feature of socialist cultural policies.) These feats opened many doors for Kati as a touring and recording artist across Europe and beyond. Her acting in auteur films by canonical directors, such as Miklós Jancsó (*The Confrontation*) and Márta Mészáros (*The Girl*), also shaped her image as a vibrant and versatile talent.

Despite the grinding and raw energy of Kati's song as opposed to the mysticism in Bea's approach, a listen to the original and the cover of "Oh, Lord" will reveal the kinship of vocal style between the two singers. With its simple structure and five-tone melody replicating old rural musical forms, including the blues, the original "Oh Lord" may have sounded familiar to young Hungarians, since folk songs formed the Kodalyian foundation of music education.[10] Meanwhile, with its pumping hard rock sound, a nod to Rare Earth, "Oh Lord" could not have been more in tune with global trends. Kati's

---

[9][bcsaba] Interjú Sipos Péterrel. First part. *Passzió*. February 23, 2011. http://passzio.hu/proba/indexfilter.php?beta=22407 (last accessed November 8, 2020).

[10]Zoltán Kodály (1882–1967) was a key figure in twentieth-century classical music—a composer, educator, and ethnomusicologist. The music teaching method bearing his name emphasizes unaccompanied singing and the reliance on indigenous folk melodies. The method was first introduced in Hungary, developed by Kodály's colleagues and students in the mid-twentieth century, and has been internationally adopted, frequently in combination with other approaches.

ecstatic solos showed the influence of Motown and Janis Joplin. In contrast, Bea's softer rendition replaces the chugging electric guitar sound with a more intimate evocation of one's relationship with natural forces. Whereas Kati's shouts address "God" up and "out there," Bea's ornate Middle-Eastern singing style suggests the presence of the divine inside and around us.

Crystallizing a performer's individuality as a motive underlies the majority of the musical tracks on "I'll Be Your Plaything," enabling Bea and Samu to experiment with surprising instrumental arrangements, a variety of voices, and an unexpected blending of musical traditions. Let us consider two same-era pieces, the slow, swing ballad "Life Goes On" (track #8) and the iconic schlager of post-1956 Hungary "Time Stands Still" (#32). Both are romantic love songs addressing existential concerns about time, space, passion, life, and death. "Life Goes On" offers a sober breakup message to a jilted lover, while "Time Stands Still" celebrates blissful love between two people "alone with the stars." Both songs and their popularity attest to the Kádár-regime's emphasis on private life and private passions, not merely as a much needed corrective to the over-politicized 1950s, but also as a "safer" alternative to people's meaningful engagement in civic life.

The composers of "Life Goes On", Jenő Horváth and Rudolf Halász, belonged to a prolific and erudite cohort of authors of dance songs, stage, and film music in what could be called the Tin Pan Alley of Budapest during the 1930s and early 1940s. A student of Zoltán Kodály, Horváth's ambition was to earn his living as a classical music composer but, as he confessed, "in a small coffee house in Budapest I was inspired by urban folk music. It would be an uncharted path [for me] but may as well lead to high peaks."[11] He grew successful boasting authorship of sixteen of the first twenty songs ever released on a Hungarian musical record. The lyricist, Halász, worked as a producer of movie scripts, operetta librettos, and chansons, while in charge of programming in the Bar Moulin Rouge before World War Two.[12]

"Life Goes On" is a torch song recorded by pre-rock era women singers, such as Erzsi Kovács and Elsie Gallay. Life goes on and time heals the wound of a breakup, one is told, and, as the narrator suggests, "we are but dust in the universe." The persuasiveness of such bromides is eroded by a bit of drama and desperation in the middle section of the song, marked by a shift from major to minor key, and a suspended melody line. Predictably, however, the major-key melody returns with its steady swing lulling the listener (and the dumped lover) into a bittersweet acceptance.

Bea's cover begins, in Samu's words, "in relentless sadness" (Rónai 2010). But it creeps in from outside the private world of lovers, the broader societal milieu into which we take a tiny glimpse. "Life Goes On" is the last of three connected tracks: "Again, Nothing Will Happen Tomorrow" (track #6) is a non-musical fragment of a conversation lifted from the name-day celebration in which a male employee makes a solemn statement to the factory's management, alluding to some grievance of his. One or more women employees respond by giggling. "Has something happened"? the man self-consciously asks his co-workers, which

---

[11]"100 éve született Horváth Jenő" DMKR. Dublini Magyarok Közösségi Rádiója. Radio program aired on May 28, 2015. https://dmkr.info/hu/musoraink/190-100-eve-szuletett-horvath-jeno (last accessed November 20, 2020).
[12]Halász Rudolf. Forgatókönyvíró, dalszövegíró. Online Encyclopedia entry in *Hangosfilm*. https://www.hangosfilm.hu/filmenciklopedia/halasz-rudolf (last accessed November 20, 2020).

could well be the listener's question since the conflict hinted at remains hidden from us. A woman quips, "Nothing will happen tomorrow either." Does that response sound like a title for a track? To the producers it did, as they elevated it into a stoic commentary on the day-to-day realities of life in the garment factory, and perhaps, more broadly, on the anti-climactic decade of Hungarian society disillusioned in the wake of repressed economic reforms and thwarted hopes of political renewal after 1968 on top of the lingering trauma of 1956.

The next track of the sequence titled "Nothing" (#7), Samu's baroque music inspired dark-toned cello piece, augments a sense of gloom bleeding into "Life Goes On," connecting reflection on the sociopolitical with the personal realm of everyday life. Leaving the lyrics and the melody unchanged, Bea's version alters the emotional dynamic of the song. In contrast to the original's three-part symmetry, the "relentless sadness" morphs into a happier mood. Initially, the cello's repetitive motif is out-of-sync with the melody, almost independent of it. But the entering drums add oomph and swing to Bea's vocal part so that the cello gives up on its stubborn minimalism and, after a fiery run-up, it mellows into the singer's accompanist. The soundscape grows ever fuller and sunnier. Challenging the fatalism of the original song, Bea's version accentuates the liberating aspect of moving on from a broken relationship with a genuine smile. A light-hearted, traditional jazz-style instrumental version of "Life Goes On" reinforces this message toward the end of the album (track #30).

The original version of "Time Stands Still" (composed by András Bágya and György G. Dénes) is linked with two prominent radio stars, the crooner János Vámosi, Hungary's response to Frank Sinatra, and the classically trained Ilona Hollós. The song's cozily conventional melody—especially when enhanced by Vámosi's ingratiating baritone—and its waltzy rhythm, delivers a message about the sublime found in the intimacy of coupledom—a perspective harshly condemned as petit-bourgeois by hardline ideologues before 1956. In 1982 the song was brought back to public focus by the eponymous cult film directed by Péter Gothár, garnering international acclaim (including Best Foreign Film of the New York Film Critics Circle Awards).[13] Dramatizing the emergence of a rebellious rock and roll culture, and its repression in the early 1960s (years before the Song Dance Festivals) amidst the Hungarian state's half-hearted efforts at liberalization, the film turned this song into a symbol of confusing and depressive times. The song thus accrued new meanings on the screen. Rather than signifying time's magical freeze for lovers, it absorbed the trauma of people to whose lives "Time Stands Still" was a soundtrack—or rather one of several soundtracks. For Hungarians, the Gothár film conveyed the message that the *historical* time of society—time meaning progress, a movement forward—came to a standstill.[14] Gryllus interpreted the song's romantic lyrical cliché, "Only you and me are on Earth," literally, imagining what this kind of aloneness and "timelessness" in the universe might *sound* like. The outcome is a dreamy, meditative, somewhat disquieting, ambient soundscape surrounding the singer's harmonically unsupported, lonely melody.

Localization. The story of "Que Sera" bespeaks to the ways translated songs take on a life of their own, becoming actors in

---

[13]See https://www.imdb.com/title/tt0082729/awards?ref_=tt_awd (last accessed January 28, 2021).
[14]The film, inevitably, reflected on its own time period of late socialism as well, which was confusing and depressing in its own unique way. Youth culture, once again, became loud and political, participating in the slow breakdown of the regime in Hungary (Szemere, 2001).

history and collective memory in a different national or cultural context. The production of unique, localized, and/or hybridized versions of international hits is part of the routine operation of the global music business, representing the third major type of covering on "I'll Be Your Plaything." The two imported songs from the US marked not only Samu and Bea's taste of their teen years but the growing prevalence of Anglo-American music Hungarians had access to via radio, records, tapes, and live events. It may not be coincidental that these two American megahits landing on the album had been recorded by such Black American stars as Stevie Wonder (track #20 "Part-Time Lover") and Whitney Houston (track #10 "My Love Is Your Love"). Asked by a reporter of which singers she felt envious and why, Bea responded that Joni Mitchell's courage as a songwriter fascinated her but she would love to "borrow" Whitney Houston's relaxed throat and high vocal sounds! (Koronczay, 2014).

The original version of "Part-Time" was a crossover: a chart-topper on Billboard Hot 100, R&B, dance, and adult contemporary. Bea and Samu had this song cross over some more genre boundaries by reinventing this R&B number—sung in English—as a jaunty blend of Balkan/Romani and Hungarian *tánchāz* (dance house) music.[15] An upbeat melody on flute provides the warm-up to an exuberant dance party,

---

[15]Following the decline of staged folklore cultivated in pre- and postwar Hungary, an urban amateur folk music revival began in the 1970s with a holistic approach to folk singing and dancing known as the dance house movement. The hard core of revivalists collected, transcribed, and performed old village music and dance with the goal of learning and teaching its language rather than imitating individual performances. With state sponsorship, the movement has built up an extensive network of clubs, fairs, summer camps, and workshops both domestically and within the Hungarian diaspora abroad. In 2011, UNESCO adopted the dance house as the "Hungarian model of the transmission of intangible cultural heritage."

where the tuba enters with the signature motif of Stevie Wonder's song accompanied by rhythmic whistling by the band members, a fixture of traditional East European folk music/dancing. Bea sings in English over a rowdy mix of talk, shouts, and singing. The overall ambience may be familiar to fans of the Serbian Boban Marković Orkestar. The surreal effect of this whirl reaches its peak with "csujogatás"—the musicians' rhythmic, often graphic sexual commentary shouted over the music—another staple of traditional folk parties employed to raise the party's "temperature."

"Part-Time" is a song about adultery, where the cheater is also cheated on, therefore the protagonist feels free to revel in its guilty pleasures. It is also about ambiguity, the questioning of rigid boundaries. To transplant this particular Western commercial pop song into a traditional folk dance party setting where Hungarian village music is mixed with Balkan Romani sounds, may be viewed as an ironic commentary on the

Figure 2 *Palya Bea's ensemble at concert.*

From right counterclockwise: Endre Kertész, János Mazura, Gábor Bizják, Mátyás Bolya, Iván Barvich, Balázs "Dongó" Szokolay.

Figure 3 *Bea and József Barcza Horváth at concert.*

ideology of folk music in Hungary and the anxiety about its boundaries. In Chapter 1 we referred to the constraints of professional folk singing and Bea's ongoing search for a less musically restrictive outlet for her talent and ambition as a singer-songwriter. The world music community, with its penchant for hybridizing musical idioms and embrace of improvisation, opened up that space for her. In re-conceiving "Part-Time," Bea, Samu, and the folk band placed unapologetic mixing and blending—of the traditional and the commercial,

Figure 4 *András Dés and Mátyás Bolya at concert.*

folk and pop, Hungarian and "other," Eastern and Western—
into the center of the song. The resulting musical piece is not
merely a delightful hybrid but the celebration of hybridity.

Houston's "My Love Is Your Love" (written and produced by
Wyclef Jean and Jerry Duplessis) is another R&B song reconceived
in a different musical idiom. It presents a vivid contrast to "Time
Stands Still," where private happiness is portrayed to exclude the
social world. "My Love" emphasizes the interconnectedness of
the personal and the intimate with the communal level of
existence. Even in the ultimate disaster scenario, as envisioned
by the narrator, the energy and sustenance gained by two
people's dedication to each other feeds on the community of

which they form a part. This idea is musically enacted by a mixed chorus taking over the melody in the refrain while Houston embellishes, joins, or responds to it. Bea's cover, sung in English, is another radical remake inspired by the distinctive folk music and dance of Gyimes, a Transylvanian village. The R&B/reggae rhythm is replaced by a slow-dance rhythm played on *ütőgardon*, a peculiar cello-shaped percussion instrument. Despite the major rearrangement, the warm soulfulness and communal feel of "My Love" has remained intact, an effect of the sensitive "translation" of the song's dramatic structure. In Houston's version, the emotional climax of the song ("I'll be waiting for you after judgement day") is followed by a celebratory communal singalong. In Bea's cover, this moment of the singer's joyful mingling with her community is accentuated by the insertion of a lively Hungarian folk tune played and sung in unisono, conjuring the spirit of happy abandon at *táncház* events. Bea's use of a "Hunglish" accent is another gesture of localization—disappointing some of her fans[16]—as is her replacement of Houston's reference to New York's Grand Central with Budapest's *Keleti pályaudvar* (Eastern Railway Station).

Irony and humor. As argued earlier, a great deal of ambiguity surrounds ironic covers, our fourth type of appropriation. Is irony intended or "merely" projected by fans? Who or what does it target in a given piece of music: a genre, a subcultural style, a specific song, its performer(s), a performance style, or some combination of all? Especially when the song lyrics are left unchanged and the humor is merely musically coded, "missing" or "getting" the irony depends on the listeners' taste, sensibility,

---

[16]See viewers' comments on "Palya Bea—My love is your love." https://www.youtube.com/watch?v=fU5wMiTZVGA (last accessed February 25, 2021).

and familiarity with the artists' musical strategies—sociologically speaking, on the listeners' cultural or subcultural capital, which in turn is shaped by a myriad of social markers, such as gender, sexuality, ethnicity, social class, age, nationality, and more. On our album, too, the intended irony may not be apparent for every listener. A kind of deadpan or absurdist humor is produced by the fragmented and decontextualized material recorded at the name-day event, its juxtaposition with musical tracks, and use as cues for the producers to reflect on broader social issues. Irony, in other words, is as much the property of the concept-album as a whole as of the individual covers.

Even so, some individual tracks, such as "Tiketike" (#1), "I Won't Be Your Plaything" (#2), "After me, the Deluge" (#5), and the multi-track "America" come across as humorous or ironic in light of the drastic or startling re-arrangements, although never parodistic. Samu and Bea emphasized that they had had no intention to ridicule the songs, their composers, performers, or their audience. In Samu's words:

> [The new instrumentation was not devised] to alter the music but to interpret it in a manner authentic to ourselves. It's hardly a pure chance, we thought, that these songs had stayed in people's memory cells. Far from it! Each song has something unique to it that accounts for its enduring popularity.[17]

The song "After me, the Deluge" (Rudolf Tomsics and Sándor Halmágyi) must have sounded quite unfashionable at the time to cover on "I'll Be Your Plaything." This is a piece about

---

[17]Palya Bea: *Én leszek a játékszered*. CD. Booklet. Translation by authors.

heartbreak and the back-and-forth between regret, defiance, and hope amplified by a blustering symphony arrangement. Winner of the second Dance Song Festival in 1967, "After Me" elevated its performer, Péter Poór, into stardom at home and across the Soviet Bloc. The ingenuity of Bea's cover lies in imbuing this oldie with the trappings of Romani folk music. On hearing this rendition, one may discover that the Gypsy musical elements had always been surreptitiously there in the original as well—with its abrupt shifts between profound sadness and boisterous merrymaking. Hungarians have an apt name for this phenomenon, "weeping while merrymaking" *(sírva vigadás)*—a peculiar trait not only of "Gypsy music"—the kind of restaurant music traditionally played by Roma string bands for the "Gadjo" (non-Roma)—but the broader national culture that "Gypsy musicking" *(cigányzenés mulatozás)* symbolizes.[18] Bea's version reveals the pop song's hidden "Gypsy" roots, but she and her musicians go a step further by turning "After Me" into a rootsy "authentic" Romani folk piece

---

[18]"Weeping-while-merrymaking" connotes a mindset carrying substantial historical baggage in Hungary where feudal structures and cultural habits survived well into the twentieth century since the mid-nineteenth century revolutionary efforts to shake off Habsburg rule and the institutions of feudalism had been defeated. "Weeping while merrymaking" originally referenced the revolutionary elite's passive resistance and melancholy state of mind because of its failure. Over the decades, this elite noble class grew impoverished, yet refused to join the capitalistic entrepreneurial classes, a large segment of which was ethnically German or Jewish. By the turn of the twentieth century, a fault line developed within the dominant culture and ideology. A backward-looking intransigent nationalism upheld by aristocrats and the gentry faced an emergent Western-oriented liberal cosmopolitanism adopted by the bourgeoisie, which however remained politically weak. Although *Gypsy music* was widely appropriated as a musical vernacular across social groups, for its critics it has symbolized a distressed national history and identity.

with added finger snapping, oral bass, and tapping on jugs. In her makeover from mainstream Gypsy music to rootsy Romani folk, Bea exaggerates the slow *hallgató* (meaning "song for listening"), and accelerates the fast and buoyant *pergető* (or spinning song played for dancing)—two fundaments of this musical idiom.[19] Recent covers of the song reveal that Bea has taken over the song's ownership from Péter Poór, which indicates not only her rendition's success, but the growing appeal of Romani folk with Hungarian audiences.[20]

In this chapter we explored the unique design of "I'll Be Your Plaything," its types of covering, and techniques of constructing a narrative via interweaving the reinterpreted schlagers with traces of the past and the present. The album has evoked two signature rituals of socialist era Hungary, the Dance Song Festival, a nationwide media spectacle, and a most ordinary ritual, the name-day celebration held by a factory's socialist brigade. Both are centered on reciting popular songs. The Festival signified the socialist "sublime," while the name-day celebration stood for the everyday, the "mundane." In weaving

---

[19]The politics of authenticity in Rom music is as complex and contested as in many other popular music genres. Folklorists and revivalists regard the music played by Roma for themselves in a communal setting as "authentic" as opposed to the restaurant music associated with professional Romani musicians. "Authentic" Romani music furthermore is produced by the Vlach and Boyash sub-groups of Hungarian Roma, whereas "Gypsy music" is typically performed by the more assimilated Romungros. With the rise of Rom folk revival in the 1970s, however, the music has been staged and performed for ethnically mixed audiences as an expression and politicization of Rom identity. It has furthermore been adopted by non-Roma musicians across various music genres (György 2020).

[20]See, for instance, Opitz Barbi's (https://www.youtube.com/watch?v=h2SZowbrcJc) and Singh Viki's (https://www.youtube.com/watch?v=3YXcNMF_yxs) covers of the song (last accessed February 25, 2021).

them together, the listener is presented with a more layered and nuanced story than typical postsocialist retrospections. It, however, would remain incomplete without elaborating on another crucial theme of the album: Bea's play with, and versions of, femininity, to be addressed in the next chapter.

5 "A Babe in Toyland" or Popcultural Feminism in Bea Palya's Music and Early Career (2005–2014)

The title of this chapter refers to the pioneering all-female rock band from Minnesota *Babes in Toyland*, which in turn took its name from a famous operetta (Victor and MacDonough 1903). *Babes in Toyland* performed intermittently, with changing lineups, from 1986 until their recent breakup in 2020 (Karlen 1994). The theme of playing music and playing with music is a central feature of "I'll Be Your Plaything." A "babe in Toyland," as we chose to describe Bea's portrayal on the album cover and attached booklet, invokes a mythical figure of femininity in modern Western cultural history, and an object of fascination in works such as Henrik Ibsen's *A Doll's House,* the classic Hollywood film *The Blue Angel* starring Marlene Dietrich, or Marge Piercy's poem *Barbie Doll* (see Figure 5). The sexualized stereotype has been exploited by icons of pop culture history, including Marilyn Monroe, Madonna, Katy Perry, and the protagonist in the Aqua music video "Barbie Girl." Closely associated with the term "girl," with its own complex set of connotations (Whiteley, 2005 65–70), the doll's figure primarily signifies the male fantasy of a sex object who is borderline underage. Yet, because of its often critical, self-reflective, or parodistic uses by female pop

Figure 5 *Bea revisiting her childhood. CD booklet.*

artists—even the aforementioned ones—the doll carries no fixed or unambiguous meanings.

Adult fashion dolls, such as Barbies, have the dubious, although not uncontested, reputation of building young girls' aspirations of becoming, first and foremost, sexualized bodies,[1] while baby dolls are typically viewed as instrumental in preparing them for the role of primary caregiver in a nuclear family. In the photograph of what seems Bea's childhood bedroom (pictured on the unfolding booklet attached to the album), we see the apparently incongruous image of her as an adult woman putting on lipstick while facing her former companions. She had several baby dolls but not Barbies because they were rare in Hungary at the time: a plush bear, books, a reel-to-reel tape recorder, flowers, and a few pieces of bijoux. This unmistakably female space is also one of self-reflection connecting the personal with the social, the child with the woman, and the nostalgic with the satirical. How did Bea's play as a girl and how did the songs she listened to on her tape recorder prepare her to play as an artist with the dominant

---

[1]For a cultural analysis of Barbie as an icon, see Rogers (1999) and for an example of Barbie's localization, see Yaqin, A. (2007).

norms of femininity in a cultural milieu resistant to gender critique? Palya's career, persona(s), and creative work, we will suggest, represent a local version of popcultural feminism. After defining this concept, we will look at the various aspects of Bea's gender critique as a singer-songwriter carving out her space in the popular music world and performing her version(s) of femininity through the songs on "I'll Be Your Plaything."

5.1. What is Popcultural Feminism?

This broad and evolving concept covers a wide range of expressive styles and cultural practices that critically engage with gender and sexuality (for example, Gauntlett 2004; Zeisler 2008; Smith-Prei and Stehle 2016; James 2020). We consider it synonymous with *popfeminism* as applied by Carrie Smith-Prei and Maria Stehle to survey multiple local and global events, activism, and feminist-driven work in pop and fine art. The term *popular feminism* is also common where the emphasis is on the commercial and expressive aspects of feminist-driven popculture (James 2020, 2–8). Overall, the relationship between pop culture and feminism(s) is quite conflicted (Zeisler 2008), but most critics agree that the former is a vehicle for making feminist critique relevant and relatable for broad segments of society. Through engagement with gender-conscious popculture, women are encouraged to defy restrictive beauty standards, reclaim ownership of their body, and redefine it as a site of pleasure and dignity. The best of this kind of popculture—much of which has been produced and not merely performed by women from rom-coms to television shows and pop music—offers tools and strategies for women to navigate everyday life at the workplace, in personal and public spaces shaped as they still are by patriarchal, homo- and transphobic and racialized social structures. Pop culture is a terrain where dominant gender and sexual relations are incessantly questioned, subverted, debated, and negotiated (Whiteley, 2005). Importantly, it is also a terrain where the logic of capitalist commoditization, glitz, and spectacle easily co-opts messages of female empowerment into a brand or gimmick (James 2020).

Women in pop *music* have been paramount partly because, as Jennifer Keishin Armstrong (2017) in Billboard has noted, its concern with sexuality makes pop divas "more relevant to our perception of gender roles than any other kind of entertainer—or public figure." Whether seen as educators or entertainers, victims or goddesses, the influence of stars such as Tina Turner, Aretha Franklin, Madonna, Taylor Swift, Beyoncé, or Lady Gaga to promote awareness about violence inflicted on women, social injustice, harassment, plain old sexism, and homophobia is difficult to overestimate. Popcultural feminism, however, is not only about songs, but also about the institutional and cultural spaces and positions that women obtain within an industry that, historically, has stereotyped and marginalized them (for recent examples see Barna 2017, Raine and Strong 2018, Csóka et al. 2018). The concept moreover includes all those business moves and media strategies that enable women artists to balance between demands of credibility and integrity, on the one hand, and having an impact on a larger audience, on the other.

Whereas women in punk (Patti Smith, Nina Hagen, the Riot Grrrls, or the Hungarian intermedia artist Kriszta Nagy [Tereskova]) gained fame or notoriety with more hard-edged or even outrageous styles of gender critique than glamorous pop divas (Juno 1996, O'Brien 1995), Madonna's sophisticated and provocative performances and savvy moves as a business woman in the 1990s elicited the greatest, though not uncontested, fascination among academic feminists, despite the fact that she rarely, if ever, has identified herself as a feminist (Fouz-Hernandez and Jarman-Ivens 2004). David Gauntlett attributes four key themes to Madonna: the celebration of popular feminism; women as confident sexual agents; fluid identities and the reinvention of the self, and, finally, being comfortable with contradictions and transformations (168). As well, unlike punk and queer women parodying hegemonic femininity, Madonna, her popfeminist "sisters" and "daughters" (Britney Spears, Miley Cyrus, Nicki Minaj, and others), seldom have deviated from dominant beauty standards and pop appeal. Contemporary debates regarding pop's affective and effective gender work therefore still revolve around the tension between mass popularity and individual commercial success, as opposed to the social-critical thrust of gender and sexual politics and the integrity of creative work.

The global spread of popcultural and movement feminisms has provoked drastic repercussions on a global scale. In postsocialist countries, such as Hungary and Poland where feminism has had barely any traction before, the backlash was particularly damaging. Back in the 1990s, Edit András's (1995) sensitive analyses of gender discontent uncovered in the works of Hungarian women artists, most of whom had refused to define themselves in feminist terms, stirred considerable controversy. Consciously or not, these artists eschewed the verbal rhetoric of gender critique in fear of ghettoization and devaluation of their art. This situation has barely improved, if at all, over the past decades. Because of the growing repressive sway of patriarchal populist nationalism in the twenty-first century, especially since the re-election of Viktor Orbán's Fidesz party in 2010, feminist thought and movements in Hungary have been increasingly relegated to the fringes of the cultural and intellectual landscape, to the pockets in academia and left politics and subcultures (Kováts 2018, Pető 2020). Feminist concerns and mainstream popularity have turned into veritably mutually exclusive concepts. So, then, how successfully could Bea bring them into proximity with each other?

5.2. Charting a Path of her Own

On the album Bea covers a song titled "The Ballad of Blond Annie" (*Szőke Anni balladája*, # 27), composed by two celebrated beat musicians (Lajos Illés and János Bródy) and first performed in 1967 by a leading folk-pop singer, Zsuzsa Koncz.[2] The "Ballad" is of interest for its gender sociological implications. It chronicles the story of a village girl who, lured by the big city's lights and the prospect of a more modern life, left her home. But instead of thrill and happiness, she found drudgery and loneliness in that big city. With its folky flavor and multi-part vocals, "The Ballad" was among the most musically appealing and memorable songs of the Illés and Zsuzsa Koncz.

---

[2]Similarly to folk singers such as Joan Baez or the young Judy Collins, Koncz cultivated a kind of femininity that sought to divert attention from the physical body to the meaning and politics of the performed songs. Koncz's pleasing yet unadorned appearance has lent credibility and an intellectual sheen to her persona. The lyrics of her songs born during the socialist era contained political commentary via double entendre. Like Baez's live performances, Koncz's sing-along "anthems" have also galvanized arena audiences, most notably, her acoustic folk-based "If I were a rose" (*Ha én rózsa volnék*), composed and at times "covered" by János Bródy, a protest song occasioned by the aforementioned military crackdown on the Czechoslovakian reform movement of 1968.

Breaking away from the conventional major/minor harmonies and guitar-band arrangement, it used modal harmonies and folk instrumentation, which not only elevated the music's respectability, but also lent it a fresh countercultural sound associable with the blending of Celtic musical elements in with Anglophone folk rock.[3]

The lyrical message of "The Ballad," however, was not particularly countercultural, let alone feminist, if not for the fact that it related a girl's story with great sympathy—itself a rarity, given the sexist and misogynist tendencies of Hungarian rock music (Kürti 1991, 2012; Szemere 2000, Barna 2017, Csóka et al. 2018). More covertly, the ballad sent a message to young women to keep their ambitions low and avoid taking risks. Surprisingly for a beat musical piece, it echoed the discourse of Women's Weekly (Nők Lapja), the official press organ of socialist Hungary's only women's organization. In this magazine, as Eszter Zsófia Tóth (2010) has pointed out, the motives and life stories of uneducated and unmarried young women moving to industrial cities had comprised a long-running narrative. Typically portrayed as vulnerable for lacking a man's protection in the home, the protagonists of the reports were portrayed as prone to going "loose," ending up as prostitutes or unwed mothers. Although written by, for, and about women, Women's Weekly failed to offer anything more than teary sentimentalism to these girls, and neither did "The Ballad."

---

[3] The best-known recording of "The Ballad of Szőke Annie" by Koncz may be viewed in an excerpt of the iconic film addressing the 1960s youth culture entitled *Ezek a fiatalok* ["These Youths"] See "Ezek a fiatalok (Banovich Tamás, 1967, részlet)" https://www.youtube.com/watch?v=sML9uUw_uoc (last accessed September 7, 2021).

Bea's cover of the song highlights the autobiographical elements of the narrative of "I'll Be Your Plaything." The girl whose bedroom we see on the album booklet is leaving her dolls and relatively safe childhood behind for the unknown. At a live performance Bea introduced the song by stating that as a village girl her own story had set off like Annie's and could have easily ended up as a fiasco as well. "Fortunately, however," she added, "my life took a different direction."[4] By embellishing the vocal melody as characteristic of Hungarian folk singing and throwing a few more folk instruments into the mix, Bea's version amplified the folk at the expense of the rock component of the ballad. By doing so, she added a meta-commentary on her musical roots and early career as a folk singer and dancer.

Bea never heeded the ballad's message, however, and devised a daring path for herself. In Chapter 1 we followed her musical career from participating in several musical groups and collective projects through the release of *Psyché*, the album. And even though *Psyché* earned Bea the coveted recognition as a musical artist, the search for a path of her own continued to entail personal struggle, self-questioning, and an ongoing intellectual and emotional investment into her domestic and international career (Palya 2011, Szentgyörgyi 2019). Figuring out her niche at the intersection of folk, world music, pop, and the singer-songwriter tradition, she gained increasing control over her creative output and career. Although, in general, she avoided the "f-word" (feminism), her rhetoric in the pop field was, and still is, rather unique, with its

---

[4]See "Palya Bea—Szőke Anni balladája," https://www.youtube.com/watch?v=ckKbdiTdAll (last accessed February 2, 2021).

sharp gender critical focus, highlighting the disparities not only regarding the current condition and structures of the music industry, but also its history. She talked with sympathy about the earlier generation of women vocalists who she thought had desired to write their own songs but couldn't overcome the obstacles. Bea, at the same time, sensed that there was a moment for change; that she could realize her ambitions with a new voice and image of femininity in a way that had not been possible for her predecessors decades earlier. And while her discontent and restlessness was genuine, Bea also knew how to make the best use of these impulses in her narratives, refashioning her persona in which "creative," "popular," and "woman" carried equal weight.

As well, while preferring to make music with men, she sought out and benefited abundantly from collaborations with women in the music industry. She went to great lengths to connect rather than collide with female vocalists in her

Figure 6 *Bea at the press conference of I'll Be Your Plaything.*

field.[5] Her managers have been women who often became close friends and co-creators. The French, Juliette Camps, who had spent many years in Hungary for her infatuation with Hungarian folk singing, worked not only as her manager but her record publisher as well. She was "like an older and wiser sister," encouraging Bea to experiment boldly with performance formats, voices, and transgress boundaries (Palya ibid. 127–8). She hosted Bea's house concerts; as a manager stood behind Bea's first solo album (*From Branch to Branch*, 2003) and unaccompanied stage performances, which resulted in the album *Justonevoice* (2009) straddling the divide between old Hungarian and Eastern European ballads and modern compositions of her own that defy categories. *Justonevoice* was also a first for Bea, to have taken care of every aspect of the creative process—from concept to execution and from engineering to liner notes. In the period between *Psyché* and "I'll Be Your Plaything," Bea continuously toured at home turning out an album yearly with an increasing number of her own songs.[6] After working with small specialized record companies, in 2008 she signed up with Sony Music releasing four albums, including "I'll Be Your Plaything."

Exoticization, folk authenticity, and commercial popularity have been three pivotal issues Bea had to tackle in order to create a relatively unencumbered space for herself. In a conference talk, Barbara Rose Lange (2020) claimed that "female performers of Hungarian world music have not only captured a unique opportunity for musical expression but for

[5]Authors' interview with Palya and Gryllus, February 13, 2020.
[6]For a more detailed list of Bea's tours in Europe and the US, as well as her awards from the Hungarian government and the music industry, see Lange 2018 and Palya 2011.

expression of femininity." Assessing the accomplishments of Irén Lovász and Ági Szalóki, Lange has pointed to the innovative and resourceful manner these world-music singers have managed to reshape the male-defined characteristics of the genre (especially the buoyancy linked with Balkan/Roma music). Lovász has brought her ethnographic expertise and concern with female-healing power in traditional folk culture to bear on her artistry. Szalóki, after leaving behind the romping Balkan/Roma band Besh-o-Drom, has built a solo career engaging, besides folk, in children's music, cabaret, and light jazz. Restraint, Lange concludes, is the shared feature of these singers' projects and Palya's gentle mode of traversing musical genres and realms displays the same tactic.[7]

Restraint for some revivalists, however, may be a tactic of self-defense, in our view, in the regimented cultural world of folk music rather than an aesthetic expression of individuality. And Bea's persona(s) can't be properly described with gentleness. Although consciously seeking peace and harmony in her personal and professional networks, she has rocked more than one boat with her frank and flamboyant display of female sexuality, as well as her struggles to negotiate her image and style with the representatives of the music business.

In her memoir, she tells a story of exoticization, an obvious pitfall for a Hungarian artist espousing her Romani background abroad. The Bea Palya Quintet was responsible for making music in the French-Romani filmmaker Tony Gatlif's *Transylvania*. Besides the thrill and prestige involved in working with an acclaimed director, singing and acting on film seemed like an ingenious mode of reaching a larger international audience. The experience of shooting *Transylvania* proved disappointing,

---

[7]Lange cites Rónai's characterization of Bea's projects as deconstructive.

however, throwing light on the power imbalance impairing so many collaborations between Western and Eastern European artists and institutions in popular music (Lange 2018, Elavsky 2011). Bea resented being treated as "an indigenous Roma woman from the Balkans," an image that stuck even after the shooting of the film throughout her onerous dealings with the French record company Naïve putting out her album *Adieu les complexes*. In her words:

> Naïve was predisposed to emphasize the Roma-exotic part of me. But my strength is not Balkan *exotica*. I didn't want the Gatlif-film to offer the main theme of the French promotion and my image to be built around my Romani descent.
>
> Palya ibid. 181

From attempting to leave Bea out of pivotal aesthetic decisions in the course of the album's production, to dragging its feet with delivering the product, the company made her feel like "the lowest ranking worker of a big bloated factory," striving for her rights and at times simply to be communicated with (Palya ibid. 182).

More battles had to be fought on the domestic music market where, as discussed earlier, the folk revival community's definitions of authenticity have, historically, stifled freer and eclectic uses of tradition to articulate modern sensibilities. Folk singers are reported to warn each other jokingly: "Be careful, the folk police will come and get you"! (Nagy-Sándor and Berkers, 412). In her song entitled "Smartasses" (*Megmondók*), set to a simple and well-known folk tune, Bea voices her frustration over friendly advice from friends, family, and critics, including those who seem to know better how to sing folk music. She responds defiantly, in rhyming (Hungarian) words:

They dare to tell me that "tradition is tradition"
"Sing as if you were my two-hundred-year-old granny"
I love folk songs but will contest your idea
Fancy that even my granny was once young and cheeky.

trans. A.S.

In questioning a view of tradition that fossilizes folk culture, Bea manages to bridge the generation gap between herself and her imaginary grandmother in the name of gender solidarity and irreverence. She refuses to treat the "200-year-old granny" whose recorded voice she had studied to become a revivalist as a source of sacred art to be reproduced by successive generations. After all, that "granny" may once have been another irreverent woman breaking the taboos of her time.

After signing up with Sony Hungary, Bea, whose off-the-mainstream position was a principled choice to sustain a measure of aesthetic autonomy, had to confront a highly regulated major company's expectation of popularity. She remembers that "at first, I wouldn't believe that a multinational's director would even be interested in my music since I'm not making pop and not shooting for big sales numbers" (205–6). Not coincidentally, it was Margit Geszti, another female personnel at Sony Music Hungary who contacted Bea after her concert. Bea remembers that Margit "listened to and interpreted my songs [. . .] and presented me with a bunch of ideas about how to reach a broader audience with this kind of music" (Palya, ibid. 206). Her professionalism and enthusiasm helped to dispel Bea's initial apprehension of becoming mistreated again. Assessing the four years with the company as a worthwhile experience, Bea reflected, nonetheless, on their clashing visions and methods of producing success, which at times "stretched our abilities to communicate with each other" (Palya ibid. 206). In the song Smartasses she asserts her position on how far she is willing to bend for making it big:

> They dare to tell me "You'll be famous one day
> If you talk and sing to please everyone"
> To which I repeat what the old ditty says
> (The world has barely changed since then)
> "The one who believes this is a big ass."

trans by A.S.

Arguably, Bea has managed to become and stay popular on her own terms. In 2014 she started her record label, Palya Bea Productions, an act marking a milestone in a popular musician's career even in the Internet era. Part of her success is premised on her visibility on traditional and social media. She has been engaging in ceaseless conversations with her fans, inviting them to share their thoughts and sentiments about a range of topics, from more abstract ones, such as "freedom" or "fear," to issues such as working life, divorce, parenting, and more.

In the remaining part of this chapter we will return to Bea's "doll house" to delve into the musical articulations of popfeminist themes and perspectives on the album.

5.3. Gender Themes on "I'll Be Your Plaything"

With their album, Bea and Samu brought a fresh gender-aware voice into the mainstream of local pop music. The title track, "I

Won't Be Your Plaything," represents the thematic heart of the album, and thus a web of significations is woven around girlhood, femininity, and the mother-daughter relationship ("Babe,""Mom,""Honey Hearts'"), with themes such as the grown girl's refusal to be played with ("I Won't Be Your Plaything"); her desire to stay free rather than marry the wrong guy, or marry at all ("You can't fall asleep next to me," "I don't wanna marry at all costs").

Whereas the album's pop songs (with the exception of "The Ballad of Blond Annie") conjure the private world of coupledom and familial relationships, the archival segments, as discussed earlier, let us peek into the world of women's working life and their nexus with men. This is remarkable not simply because the latter domain is conventionally outside of pop songs' thematic scope, but because, given women's full employment, their presence in workplace collectivities ("socialist brigades") constituted a salient aspect of the ideology and policy concerns of the workers' state. Women's overall social situation mattered, despite its patriarchal framing and controversial realities. By including snippets of the recordings in the garment factory—in spite of the opaqueness of the who, what, and why of the conversations—the album's producers make a meta-commentary on gender relations in socialist-era Hungary.

5.3.1. Who is playing?

The word "baba" has triple meanings in the Hungarian language: doll, infant, and—in an archaic rural idiom—lover; this polysemy is ingeniously exploited for subtle connections to be built between the individual songs and adding new layers of meaning to them. For instance, "I Won't Be Your

Plaything" is introduced by the enigmatic "Tike," a minimalist twenty-three second piece, which musically elaborates on the album cover's visual image of Bea playing with a vintage doll. She is cooing and babbling the words "tike" (deriving from the female name Esztike) and "baba," and whispering, in the old-fashioned formal address, "Be my baby. Tonight."

Unrecognizably to most listeners, "Tike" covers a lesser known "sramli" (Viennese entertainment music), dating back to the early twentieth century, entitled "Esztike girl."[8] As a marching song it survived into World War Two to be rediscovered in the 1990s by the so-called "wedding (lakodalmas or mulatós) rock" musicians, growing enormously popular by rejuvenating Gypsy music, magyarnóta, and other popular songs played at weddings with modern pop/rock instrumentation (Lange 1996). In "Esztike girl," the ebullient spirit of village fairgrounds and alcohol-soaked festivities is evoked with an old-fashioned suitor—the singer—entreating Esztike to be his baby [baba] "tonight." Bea's version could be called a modernist elliptical musical allusion to the song rather than a pop cover. It subverts the song's subject position by giving the words "be my baby tonight" into a woman's mouth who happens to be playing with a doll. But who is she and on whose behalf is she speaking? Does the adult woman reminisce about her younger self? Or does a young girl anticipate growing up and being seduced by those words? To complicate all this, the babbling and cooing may also refer to her playing with an imagined or future baby, and perhaps a

---

[8]Thank you, Samu Gryllus for directing us to the original song "Esztike, tike". E-mail communication, February 16, 2020. For a recording see "Doroszlói Rezesbanda—-Esztike lány" https://www.youtube.com/watch?v=mjloTH_8oZ0 (last accessed June 11, 2021).

lover. A whole repertory of typical gender roles (mother, lover, daughter) is condensed into this track, providing a clever prelude to the album's central concern.

"Tike" bleeds into the title track "I Won't Be Your Plaything." As the winner of the first Dance Song Festival in 1966, this unabashedly passionate piece with its grand melodic gestures and a heavy pumping beat, became, in a way, the face of that festival, turning the twenty-two-year-old singer Kati Kovács into a household name. Kati straddled the fault line between two musical worlds: Anglo-American beat music and traditional Hungarian schlager informed by Mediterranean (predominantly Italian) and German popular songs. Like Zsuzsa Koncz, she belonged to the beat generation stepping in front of a national audience after rehearsing Little Richard's songs with a guitar band in high school and imitating Ella Fitzgerald's vocals.[9] Typically, however, she couldn't have achieved fame without partnering with the representatives of the established popular music business and adopting their favored musical idiom. The success of "I Won't Be" epitomized this generational and musical interface. The song's arrangement was pompous and *estrade*-like, but Kati's gravelly vocal delivery signaled the infiltration of African-American stylistic features into mainstream Hungarian pop. (By the 1970s, the genre contours of beat and schlager became blurrier.)

Besides the overwhelmingly positive public response, Kati's rendition of the song engendered criticism and even ridicule. In it an angry young woman feels deceived and confronts her sweet-talking boyfriend, not merely on account of her romantic

---

[9]*Wayback Machine. Internet Archive.* "Kovács Kati: énekes, szövegíró, színésznő. Életrajz" Online. https://web.archive.org/web/20120210221348/http://www. kovacskati.hu/Career/career.html (last accessed February 3, 2021)

expectations but also her dignity. The vocal articulation of her passion was unappealing to many. "If someone can sing this well, why would they need to shout"? was a recurrent reaction from older listeners (cited by Dalos 2015: 4). As well, the close-up view of Kati's serious, smileless face did not meet conventional mass audience expectations set towards female performers. In everyday conversations it was common to remark, jokingly or with revulsion, on Kati's "bulging veins," as she sang the emotionally climactic refrain. The relatively raw physicality of her performance disturbed the narrow and sexist definitions of public decency and female attractiveness. In her essay on young pop divas making their national debuts on the Dance Song Festival in the late 1960s, Anna Dalos (ibid.) observes the emergence of a type of woman unwilling to play by the rules of patriarchy, insisting on being in charge of her life. The songs they performed were more or less banal than others, but for these singers the primary vehicle of asserting themselves was their distinctive rock and soul-flavored vocal delivery, their shout of defiance.

In 1983, the punk-legend Feró Nagy and his band, Bikini, came up with a parody of Kati's song, serving as a crucial mediator to the cover recorded on the album "I'll Be Your Plaything," since Samu had not even known the original before hearing the parody! The minimalist hard-driving punk/metal number counters Kati's in every possible manner with its repetitive narrow-range melodic riffs, fast-paced pummeling rhythm, Feró's sinister distorted vocals, and the mangled refrain. The piece may easily be heard as a misogynistic upbraiding of a "chick" who refuses to be mistreated by men— Feró's ultra-masculinist posturing definitely allows for that interpretation. Alternately, the song may simply be regarded as a sendup of a socialist-era smash hit and the show business it symbolized; the one which dismissed Feró's brand of angry outspoken working-class rock twelve years later.[10]

Redirecting her protest at sexism, Bea's cover version is an uproarious blend of folk, punk, and free jazz where she is the one playing. The introduction by the viola's slow off-beat pulse takes the listener, once again, to a *táncház* (dance house) party, but the accompanying chords are "off," and we are denied the expected harmonic resolutions at the end of the lines. More surprise is to follow. In the middle section, Bea bursts into a more-than-a-minute long ecstatic railing with the obsessively shrieked and screamed no's (*nem*)—prompting her instrumentalists to tease, counter, or emulate her in a raucous improvisational stretch. After this excuse for a refrain, Bea's singing of the verse is picking up speed over the frenzied hard driving drum as she begins to bicker with a "male" tuba. Finally, as the nerves calm down, the viola is back with a slow off-beat rhythm pattern, but the chord sequences continue to be "off," pulling the ground from under the imaginary dancers' feet in this delirious mix of genres.

The rearrangement affords a wider spectrum of affect than the original version—from nostalgia and sadness through the eroticism of dogged negation and wild skirmish between lovers to the woman's final affirmation of control. In describing how the original song was revamped, Bea explained that while "Kati's song depicted an angry chick who was duped, we added a dramatic change to the character: A naive rural girl remembers the romantic moments but then just loses it and tells her man with feminist assertiveness to bugger off" (cited by Rónai 2010).

---

[10]For a recording, see "Nagy Feró és a Bikini—Nem leszek sohasem," https://www.youtube.com/watch?v=Xr4de_jFi7Y (last accessed June 11, 2021).

5.3.2. "Next to me you can't fall asleep": Sex and play

The theme of women's sexual freedom and corporeality figures on multiple levels of the album's discourse: first, through the lyrical content, second, via the musical narrative, such as Bea's ubiquitous erotic banters with her instrumentalists, and, third, through her performance style replete with vocalization and improvisation frequently mimicking the sexual act. The three levels are frequently present in the same song or track.

The spunky heroine of "I Won't Be," expressed faith in the idea of romantic love. In contrast, the protagonists of "Next to me you can't fall asleep" (#13) and "I don't wanna get married at all costs" (#15), celebrate sexual license, disregarding rigidly conceived gender roles and demeaning stereotypes. Both songs sound off skepticism about romantic love and compulsory (heterosexual) marriage. These protofeminist songs, similarly to "Life Goes on," are rooted in the musical theater and cabaret world of pre-World War Two Budapest (even though both were composed at the turn of the 1960s) and have enjoyed a legendary status ever since. Their favor with generations of Hungarian audiences owes a great deal to the late Irén Psota (1929–2016), one of the country's preeminent theatrical and filmic talents. Her persona so powerfully defined these songs that few performers have taken up the challenge of re-recording them.[11] "Next to me"

---

[11]For the recordings, see "Psota Irén -Én mellettem elaludni nem lehet," composed by Tibor Polgár, lyricist Szilárd Darvas. https://www.youtube.com/watch?v=mJq22LYO_g8 and "Én nem akarok mindenáron férjhez menni," composed by Zdenko Tamássy, lyricist Szilárd Darvas, https://www.youtube.com/watch?v=0Hug6RvfGmY (last accessed June 12, 2021).

first appeared in a 1959 film comedy *Up the Slope* as a stage act of a "loose" cabaret singer boasting of her sexual appetite. The character was devised to represent, in the official parlance of the time, bourgeois decadence. This is how the songwriter Tibor Polgár (1907–1993) remembers the discord between his satirical intent and the audience's response:

> In the movie there was a bar scene where the young lady was to perform a cringeworthy *schlager*. With my excellent co-writer Szilárd Darvas, we put our heads together trying to produce a song with the cheapest melody and stupidest words to parody the entire genre rife with cookie-cutter songs and affected performers. In the film's leading role was Erzsi Házy, the great opera singer for whom I wrote some complex, yet pleasing, songs, which she delivered beautifully. But these songs didn't resonate with the audience [...]. In contrast, the song "Next to me you can't fall asleep, I must be loved day and night," turned out to be a smash hit. I'm still uneasy about this "success".
>
> Polgár 1980, trans. A. S.

Polgár's reflection speaks volumes about the audience's fatigue with the over-politicization and prudery of entertainment in post-1956 Hungary, prompting them to identify with the "wrong" character portrayed with the "wrong" kind of music.[12]

---

[12]Composers at times took advantage of the disconnect between ideological doctrines and audience taste by inserting jazzy or rock and roll segments with the intent to characterize "negative" types and, simultaneously, lure the audience to a show. Polgár, who a few years after writing this song emigrated to Canada to establish himself as a classical composer, was not one of them.

The twin song of "Next to me" on the album is "I don't wanna get married," a less risqué knock-off composed for Psota by Zdenko Tamássy (1921–1987) emboldened by the reception of "Next to me." It features a similarly clownish, pseudo-naïve type who lists many pitfalls of a hasty wedlock, leading one to believe that she merely postpones it in her noble quest to find "the only true one." But, in the end, she sneakily undercuts this perception to admit that she may not want a spouse at all! The use of a Caribbean rhythm, fairly uncommon in local popular music, adds eccentricity and exoticism to her figure.

To revitalize these schlagers fifty years later posed peculiar problems. How to address marriage and sex for twenty-first century women and men, who are far less inclined to wed or do so much later in life than their grandparents?[13] In "Next to Me," Bea's singing and gestures are playful and alluring without emulating her predecessor or offering a major interpretation. The song's eroticism is conveyed through gabbing between the vocal and the instrumental lines musically enacting versions of masculinity—some by supporting or embellishing the vocals, others taking the lead away from her. With a vigorous melodic line the tuba "keeps talking," even in defiance of Bea's line: "I want the one who barely talks"!

The most striking feature of Bea's Bollywood-style cover of "I don't wanna get married," is its exuberance, breaking down the

---

[13]The rate of new marriages in Hungary was decreasing over the period between 1990 and 2010, but has been steadily growing since then, partly because of the rising trend of re-marrying. Meanwhile, the age of the first marriage for both men and women steeply increased between 1990 and 2018, from 24.5 to 32.8 for men and from 21.8 to 30.1 for women (https://www.ksh.hu/stadat_files/nep/hu/nep0016.html), along with the number of unmarried cohabiting couples. See also Womanstats Project, http://www.womanstats.org (last accessed October 14, 2020).

conventional four-line structure of the song and seeking outlet in improvisatory musical materials, lengthy vocalizations, and even inserting a *konnakol*—the vocal utterance of percussive syllables with accompaniment on the tabla. As usual, Bea is a dynamic partner in the ensemble rather than its exclusive focus. But what does this joyous rendition signify regarding the marriage issue? It is safe to assume that staying a single woman entailed far less anxiety for Bea's generation than for women half a century before. Psota had to act clownish to "sell" her message, whereas Bea could simply perform her buoyant and self-confident femininity. Other interpretations are also plausible. In an essay, Rónai (2017: 106) proposed that the distance perceived in Bea's playful, at times chuckling, delivery of the song's words signals that the notion of "women not having to rush into marriage in the modern world" is old and may have been old even at the time when Psota first introduced the song to her audience. If one goes by this interpretation, the implication is that too little progress has occurred over the decades and women's social problems continue to be real.

The lascivious prelude track to "Next to Me" entitled "Schlaflied" (German for "lullaby") disrupts the concept—if anything, Schlaflied is an anti-lullaby. Over the frenzied polyrhythms of a Balkan/Roma brass band reminiscent of the Serbian Boban Marković Orkestar, Bea vocalizes with escalating heat and abandon. The track is a self-quote from a song from Weöres' *Psyché* titled "To a Groom" [Egy lovász fihoz].[14] In it the poetess laments over her lover falling asleep too soon after sex, leaving her desire unquelled. Bea's vocal line is mimicking the aroused poetess struggling with her lover—personified by a saxophone—losing stamina. In Schlaflied, Bea does not let

---

[14] Email communication with Samu Gryllus, September 29, 2020.

her man go to sleep, similarly to the cabaret singer who brags about this in the track "Next to Me." Bea's moaning signifies not simply her desire, but her need to secure fulfillment from her partner, a salient feminist concern rarely finding expression in popular music.[15]

5.3.3. Mothers and daughters

Around the time Bea gave birth to her first daughter in 2012, she became intensely interested in the intergenerational chain, shared wisdom, and solidarity connecting women of different ages and historical times (Rónai 2014). Another source of this interest came from her intimate knowledge of folk and traditional music rooted in a less individualized social world where families are multi-generational and close-knit. On the album I'll Be Your Plaything, traces of this broader concern are present through the selection of vintage pop songs on the topic, such as "Mama" (along with its prelude titled "Baba") or Bea recording a duet with her mother, titled "Mézesszívek" (Honey hearts). "Mama" was one of the three first prize-winning songs of the 1968 Dance Song Festival (also recipient of the Audience's Award) associated with another mini-skirted young talent, Zsuzsi Mary.[16] In it, a teenage girl, boasting with her 10:00 p.m. curfew, excitedly shares her experience of her first date with her mom, while seeking her permission to see the young man again, who's anxiously waiting for her outside. More than anything, the song is a paean to mothers nurturing

---

[15]On sexuality and feminist agendas, see, for example, Escoffier (2003) and Vance (1984).

[16]Composed by Attila Dobos and Iván Szenes. The television broadcast of the Festival's performance is available on YouTube: "Mary Zsuzsa—Mama" https://www.youtube.com/watch?v=OdphCI7IIhU (last accessed October 17, 2020).

their young children and, ideally, becoming their confidant in their teens. But a few lines of the lyrics sound disturbing to modern ears, such as the casual reference to what must have been standard family practice at the time: mom comforting the child after being spanked by dad. Zsuzsi's rendition is fast-paced, cheery, and danceable. Signaling her being in sync with fresh trends, she delivered the coda in a raspy "blackish" tone. (It was the first year that a beat song—by the group Illés—also ended up as a first prize winner!)

In her cover, Bea replaced the original song's speedy offbeat pulse—familiar from some Gypsy/Roma and klezmer music but amplified here by bombastic drumbeats—with a softer and more erotic Latin rhythm. There is palpable pleasure in Bea's performance of this rather silly and anachronistic song while, evidently, she sustains some distance to it. (For instance, she can't help chuckling a bit at the tired cliché in the girl's story about the movie date where she "missed" the movie.) In this way, Bea manages to wipe the dust off the song and communicate an abiding truth about mother-daughter relationships, making us realize that this invariability may itself be a source of joy.

The forty-second track titled "Honey Hearts," (track 16) represents a particularly poignant example of the mother-daughter bond. Recorded at the garment factory's name-day party, Bea's mom, Emike, is singing a *magyarnóta* (urban folk-like song) about the "honey heart" that the singer-subject of the song gave her sweetheart in order to stay in his memory. (The "honey heart", sold at village fairs, is a heart-shaped cookie covered with red food coloring and ornamented, in the Hungarian style, with icing and a tiny mirror.) Over her mother's four-line verse, Bea recorded in the studio a slow, sustained, and beautifully ornamented vocal line that stays afloat while

Emike's song reaches closure. Like Natalie Cole's 1991 duet with her father Nat King Cole, Bea's "Honey hearts" is literally a historical duet with her mother—a gift she gave to Emike. In Bea's words: "So then she hears her twenty-year-old self singing. She was then younger than me. This touched us profoundly; after all, it says 'I gave a heart to you,' and, indeed, didn't she literally give me one"? (cited by Rónai, 2010).[17]

* * *

In this chapter we portrayed Bea's feminist reappropriation of socialist-era or older songs about girlhood and womanhood, placing her inventive collaborative project with Samu Gryllus and their musical ensemble in the context of her early career within the domestic and international music business. Furthermore, in describing the album's songs in their original and cover variants, we offered a social historical perspective of the music—and its meanings—that has mattered to Hungarian people across generations.

But what is unique to Bea's popcultural feminism, and how does it speak to the broader social world largely untouched by, yet distinctly inhospitable to gender politics? First, like many other women in global pop, on this album but especially on her more recent and more gender focused recordings, she makes sure to articulate women's concerns, experiences,

---

[17]Listening to this piece might make one feel that both singers and the drone of the tanpura are somewhat independent of one another. This impression arises from Samu's compositional technique more commonly employed in art than popular music, and likely lost on most listeners: He positioned each participant's key, Bea's (D) and Emike's (G) symmetrically in regards to the H-key of the tanpura's drone so that they mirror each other and thus give a musical shape to the actual mirror placed on the honey heart. (Thank you to Samu Gryllus for sharing this information with us. E-mail communication, September 29, 2020.)

pleasures, and pains in a manner that is not alienating to men. And she achieves this not by seductive spectacles or playing on heterosexual desire. In light of users' commentaries to her videos, Bea has managed to present a distinctly female voice that seems to empower and enchant women and men alike as responses collected from YouTube users to tracks featured on I'll Be Your Plaything with gendered and "non-gendered" names testify to it:

"Greetings from the USA! Your music is a joy to me. I can't understand the lyrics, but the emotion is universal. It makes the world a smaller place. Any chance you will come to the US for a tour"?[18]

"This chick is TOP! Unbelievable how spirited her singing is"!![19]

"The lady is not here but in heaven when she is singing. How good that we have her."[20]

"I do really love Palya Bea! All the best greetings from Poland"![21]

"Gorgeous"![22]

"Thanks, Beus, I approach this song like you but a bit more swingily. This song has soul and you tuned into it so well! Respect."[23]

---

[18]User comment "Palya Bea—Szőke Anni balladája "https://www.youtube.com/watch?v=ckKbdiTdAlI. Last accessed September 8, 2021.
[19]Ibid. trans. A.S. Comment since deleted.
[20]User comment "Palya Bea—Nagy utazás (Petőfi Rádió Akusztik)" https://www.youtube.com/watch?v=J0I2e6reVmo. Last accessed September 8, 2021
[21]Ibid.
[22]Ibid. trans. A.S.
[23]Ibid. trans. A.S.

"Not only is she a talented singer. She is a Female SHAMAN"![24]

"Terribly cool."[25]

Bea may seem more cautious than her Western counterparts in presenting a voice that is *not* divisive; making sure that it is an addition rather than a corrective to or replacement of men's voices. Flirtation, breakup, or sex, as she insisted in an interview, are not female but human concerns; "thus my songs grapple with human beings' problems through a female prism" (Jankovics 2016). On the other hand, she feels passionate about balancing the dialogue between the genders, viewing herself as one breaking codes of conduct and orthodoxies in popular music production. In response to the question posed in the same interview as to whether she could be called a feminist, Bea avoided a direct answer by stating that "if by feminism you mean being hard-edged and militant, then I'm not one. I prefer gentleness and sincerity in my work. There is power in things conveyed in a firm but gentle manner; I believe these are most likely to be effective."

[24]Ibid. trans. A.S.
[25]Ibid. trans. A.S.

6   In the Aftermath of "I'll Be Your Plaything": A Woman Writing her Self

"I'll Be Your Plaything" was an outlier in terms of its marketing, reception, and its producers' musical career trajectory. It could not sell well on disk because of the absence of promotional tours. Although Bea performed several of its tracks at live shows, the large instrumental apparatus involved in the album's recording was financially and logistically forbidding to tour with.[1] This may have affected the public's response to "I'll Be Your Plaything." As seen from the YouTube views and comments, few users experience it as a carefully designed concept album; many more find and enjoy the remakes as standalone pieces with differing rates of liking and streaming. "I'll Be Your Plaything" was an outlier in terms of critical reception as well. Bea and Samu reported that, after the artistically heavy-weight *Psyché*, friends in the "high arts" seemed disappointed with the duo's turn towards "lowbrow pop," while the pop and world music community found the avant-gardist treatment of the hits alienating. This included the leading world music critic

---

[1]Interview with Samu Gryllus and Bea Palya by the authors. February 13, 2020, Budapest.

László Marton Távolodó (2010), who would have appreciated a selection of fewer schlagers with less pre- and interludes. The album, however, received stellar reviews as well, indicating that it had touched many listeners for its spirited, one-of-a-kind retrospection. Critics praised it for its "bold and unconstrained play" ([borzák] 2010); the overall harmonious effect obtained despite the complexity and stylistic diversity of the songs (Sipos 2010) or the completely new interpretation given to the overall sound of the songs and the ironic treatment of some of the obsolete lyrics (Podhorányi 2010). For Samu, "I'll Be Your Plaything" offered a rare digression from jazz and experimental music into the world of commercial pop, producing musical hybridity of an unusual kind. Bea could probe a more poppish persona with hummable tunes. In this chapter our focus will be on Bea's songwriting career and public persona unfolding in the wake of the cover album.

6.1. Writing a New Story

The detour of "I'll Be Your Plaything" drove Bea impatient to create and produce her own songs again. After releasing a live folk album of Sephardic songs titled "Thousand and one Sephardic nights" (*Ezeregy szefárd éjszaka,* Sony Music, 2012), a string of self-published releases followed. The albums "Woman/Grow" (*Nő,* 2014), "Still Woman/Grow" *(Tovább nő,* 2016),[2] "I'm finding my way home" (*Hazatalálók* 2018), and "Life" (*Élet,* 2020)

---

[2]The title of the album *Nő* plays with the double meaning of the word: "woman" and "grow", the latter referring to (psychological) growth. The next album *Tovább nő,* suggesting continuity with the former one, could be translated as "Still a woman" and "Still Grow", or by adding a comma, might as well mean something like "Woman, go farther."

showcase her confidence and skills as a songwriter and a vocalist performing with varying lineups of musicians[3] and sharing her intensely intimate experiences, desires, joys and ecstasies, lacks and longings, emotional upheavals and silences. Most pieces utilize conventional pop song structures and vernacular idioms, such as the blues, African folk music, and rap. Several key themes, compositional and performance characteristics on these albums are traceable to earlier work and are fueled by Bea's restlessness and courage to examine the world with a feminine lens beyond the thematic and poetic conventions of popular music. She reminisced:

> I was writing and performing what sounded authentic to me because the stakes were high: I needed to grow, fulfill my desires, and ultimately create a new song aesthetic and a community of listeners who would not only crave for *schlagers* but tolerate innovation as well.
>
> Szentgyörgyi 2019 trans. A.S.

Bea's urge to evolve and challenge her audience with self-composed music echoes long-standing feminist concerns about women's entry to public history through having their voice heard. For instance, the classic text, The *Laugh of the Medusa*, by the French philosopher, literary critic, poet, and playwright Hélèn Cixous (1976), opens thus: "I shall speak about women's writing: about *what it will do*. Woman must write her self. Must write about women and bring women to writing" (875). For Cixous, a poststructuralist thinker, writing is not merely a profession, a form of self-expression or self-

---

[3] Of Bea's former musicians, only István Dongó Szokolay, the wind instrumentalist, continues to play in her ensembles.

therapy, but an act of emancipation attained and furthered by stories whose authors and subjects are women. Almost as if in a dialogue with Cixous's call to arms, Bea's opening track "I'm calling you" (*Hívlak*) of her album "Woman'" is an invocation of an "imagined community" (Anderson 1983) of women—friends, relatives, known and unknown foremothers—to receive strength, nurturance, and wisdom from them necessary to effect change, "to write a new story." This song is no longer about the intimacy and complicity between mothers and daughters as portrayed in "Honey hearts'" and "Mom." And it certainly points beyond the implicated intergenerational bond Bea has formed with her predecessor, Irén Psota, by covering her cabaret songs. Yet in the song "I'm calling you," all these biological, historical, and social linkages between women are recognized and celebrated. The song is built around a richly ornamented Phrygian melody inspired by Mediterranean folk music, granting the singer's call back into the past—and ahead into the future—the kind of transhistorical sweep characteristic of Cixous's address of women who "return from afar, from always: from 'without,' from the heath where witches are kept alive" (877).

A similar idea of female solidarity is conveyed in the title track "Woman" (*Nő*) but is given a jazzy, at times, humorous rendition disrupted, though, by angry rapping in the mid-section. Protesting the demeaning or limiting stereotypes slapped onto women, Bea lists them as imagined or lived parts of her own self: the privileged and the victimized; the career woman and the trophy wife; the battered woman, the "dumb blonde," and the slut; the shy little girl and the bitter old lady. The song is a poignant expression of empathy and social commentary, and a rebellious shout against contorting conformity.

The freedom of moving between feminine roles and identities, as well as the freedom to change, Palya knows, is a dangerous proposition. Some roles have, historically, not been occupied by women (such as running a business, being a leader), while others, such as the independent (unmarried or divorced) woman embracing the idea of body- and sex-positivity run up against gendered taboos and narrow moral visions of propriety. This theme runs through all her work. Bea likes to fashion herself as a modern-day witch, a bohemian misfit who speaks her mind, dares to bare her self, and display her vulnerability without caving in to others' authority, including one's mother, teachers, bosses, and "the regime," as she cites them in her rap on the song "Woman."

In pursuing this kind of freedom, she enlists her "Gypsyness," a vital, though not preeminent part of her identity. In the song "Gypsy-like" (*Cigányos*) dedicated to her grandfather, Bea sings in the traditional musical and lyrical language of this ethnic group. She evokes tradition not to validate her ethnic otherness or folk authenticity, but something more complex: her authenticity as a modern artist ("I only sing the truth"), and her sexual freedom ("I'm a plain Gypsy slut").[4] Romani folklore also informs Bea's beloved metaphor of flying to meditate about freedom. In her commentary to the song "Two worlds" (*Két világ*) on the album "Still Woman/Grow," she relates the origins legend according to which the Roma once existed as birds. Their wings atrophied once they landed on earth and morphed into humans, but they continue to dream about taking off to the sky someday again. Flying is a state of liminality. It may mean letting go of the painful burden of the past and the

---

[4]Commentary to the track "Gypsy-like" on *Still Woman/Grow*.

anxiety about the future, enjoying the good times, the ecstasy of musicking ("Gypsy-like"). In other songs levitation assumes a metaphysical meaning as a means of transcending the realm of the earthly life and "entering a different dimension," some form of the otherworldly ("Freely" [Szabadon]" and in "Two Worlds"). A most intriguing musical treatment is given to this theme by the jittery, psychedelic, ethno-jazz piece "The flutter of wings-dream" (*Szárnysuhogás-álom*) on the album "Life," in which Bea and her superb musicians flesh out the tension between the two worlds.[5]

"By writing her self," Cixous has stated, "woman will return to the body which has been more than confiscated from her, which has been turned into the uncanny stranger on display." She sums up this argument succinctly: "Censor the body and you censor breath and speech at the same time" (ibid. 880). It is an idea that could easily be the motto of Palya's music and life philosophy. In her song "Naked with a headscarf" on the album "Life," the concept of nudity is a metaphor of her emotional sincerity as well as outspoken (and often unromantic) portrayals of sexuality. Like in the earlier song "Smartasses," Bea cites people finding fault with her music (for not fitting genre rubrics) as well as her lifestyle, although this time she seems more in control of the controversy. Making the word "nude/naked" (*meztelen*) rhyme with the word "impertinent" (*szemtelen*), Bea intimates that, in the eyes of her critics, her liberated sexuality, sincerity, and creative license are equally offensive to "good taste."

---

[5]Bea's partners are Jenő Lisztes, György Orbán, and Tamás Czirják (see discography).

As noted earlier, an internal tension in popcultural feminism lies between celebrities' adherence to restrictive norms of female beauty and their propagation of the idea of self-acceptance. In her concert and documentary film *Homecoming*, for example, Beyoncé encourages her sisters to love their bodies of whatever shape, color, and size.[6] Yet in the same film she shares with her viewers her own almost superhuman efforts to slim back into perfect shape soon after giving birth to her twins.

Bea tackles this issue in the humorous song "Mirror" (*Tükör*), where her initial self-loathing and jealousy of Barbie-bodied movie stars is giving way to self-affirmation, thanks to her mirror impersonated, though, by male vocalists saying: "You're beautiful as you are." Whether Bea thus symbolically restores the importance of the male gaze for (heterosexual) women's self-esteem is up to her listeners to decide.

The censoring of the physical body takes on many forms, including the silence about a young girl's sexual feelings and the lack of proper language to address them. In the song "What's it called?" (*Hogy hívják?*), Bea attributes this silence to women's prudery transmitted from mothers to daughters; it is a cycle she is determined to break with her child.[7] Again, we find her in conversation with Cixous on the same issue:

---

[6]*Homecoming*: A Film by Beyoncé, 2019, Parkwood Entertainment.
[7]In Bea's autobiographical songs ("Woman," "Exes," "Naked with a headscarf") and other narratives, her mother frequently represents the voice that disapproves and delimits her freedom. Feminists would interpret their conflict, as well as other (self-)oppressive practices imposed by mothers on daughters as an effect of internalized patriarchy. Bea's discord with her mother, however, is further complicated by a social class component: Bea's cosmopolitan bohemian lifestyle and liberal outlook flouts Emike's conservatism deriving from her rural working class background.

I have been amazed more than once by a description a woman gave me of a world all her own which she had been secretly haunting since early childhood. A world of searching, the elaboration of a knowledge, on the basis of a systematic experimentation with the bodily functions, a passionate and precise interrogation of her erotogeneity.

876

Palya's liberatory agenda subverts not only gendered taboos but restrictive standards of woman's normalcy. Ever since performing the Psyché character, she has consistently pushed the boundaries of popular music's thematic conventions, particularly stifling in the domestic setting, by addressing common yet momentous life experiences that women tend to go through such as pregnancy, abortion, childbirth, and motherhood. She is fully cognizant, however, that her choice of these themes may only appear subversive in the Hungarian context; her reference points are women in Western pop (Mitchell, Beyoncé, and others) who have long been disclosing such facets of their personal experiences in their music.

Whereas Bea's outspokenness may offend or baffle a conservative public, her celebration of maternity, on the contrary, may seem inadvertently apologetic to those at the opposite end of the political spectrum. In Orbán's Hungary, gender as a meaningful concept has been questioned, heteronormativity reaffirmed, and the government incentivizes women to be, first and foremost, wives and mothers.[8] In a

---

[8]In response to low birth rates and a shrinking population, the Orbán-regime, notorious for its anti-immigration policies, has devised a set of economic incentives for predominantly middle-class families to reverse current demographic trends. Meanwhile, in an attempt to delegitimize non-traditional families, new laws have been implemented to prevent LGBTQ couples from rearing children (Gorondi 2019, Walker 2020).

recent interview, Palya makes sure to dispel assumptions about her complicity with the government propaganda: "[Maternity] is not the ultimate meaning of feminine existence for everyone, other forms of female creativity are no less valuable. But to me, personally, one supreme joy of life is motherhood" (Szily, 2021). The richness of experience and self-reflection in her autobiographical songs also testifies to Bea's intent to open rather than close doors to the gamut of women's lifestyle choices. In "Exes," she relates her ending of an unhappy relationship by taking the bus and seeking to terminate her pregnancy. Written and performed in an entirely different affective register, "Once I Was Too" is a lamentation over the emotional pain of abortion. Using the archaic form of Transylvanian dance house music, the song suggests that abortion has, historically, been around for the longest time, thus contesting the conservative belief linking women's freedom of choice to modernity.

The "Birth Song" (*Szülésdal*) in contrast, is a joyous affirmation of parenthood in what seems Bea's most directly political piece to date, advocating for women's rights to determine the physical posture in which to deliver their baby rather than conforming to fossilized hospital rules. (It bears noting, that this song came out a year before Ágnes Geréb, a medical doctor pioneering the home birth movement in Hungary, was vilified and prosecuted for her activism, 2010–2012.[9]) A poetic counterpart to this song is "Human animal" (*Emberállat*) on the album "Woman," in which Bea contemplates her oneness with

[9]See Ágnes Geréb: Persecuted for Midwifery, *Frontline Defenders*, https://www.frontlinedefenders.org/en/case/agnes-gereb-persecuted-midwifery (last accessed March 20, 2021).

the animal world as her pregnant body is accommodating her growing fetus. In her words, "I'm all instinct, I'm all body/big as watermelons are my breasts and belly" (trans. A.S.).[10]

6.2. Navigating Music Making, Business, and Feminism

Early in her career Bea had an aversion towards media publicity. When working with Sony, she deleted half of the items on the press promotional list (Palya, 2011: 206). Yet, she soon learnt as the owner of Palya Bea Productions, that, to generate an audience for her off-the-mainstream music, she needed more than a Facebook profile. Over the past decade, because of her high-profile presence on non-musical and musical entertainment and print media, her name became widely recognized even among those barely familiar with her as a singer (Rónai, 2017: 100). She recently admitted that the variety of workshops she runs—on creativity, business, career development for women, and others—play nearly as significant a role in her career as music. In this extra-musical realm, she feels she capitalizes on her skills acquired as a stage performer in projecting her voice, inhabiting a space or commanding audience attention.

Bea has built an extensive total star text. The term (Dyer 1991) refers to the (self-) positioning of an artist by a careful

---

[10]The song paraphrases a classic, widely known Hungarian poem "I'll be a gardener" (*Kertész leszek*) by Attila József (1905–1937), where the poet-subject imagines seeking refuge from the noises of a war-torn, devastated Europe of the 1920s by fully dedicating himself to cultivating a garden. Without the dark overtones of that poem where a romanticized natural world is set in opposition to a social world, Bea likewise turns away from the social towards the biological realm in order to cultivate and appreciate a new life.

construction of their persona(s), image, or, to use a crasser concept, their brand across a range of media outlets. Journalists, television show hosts, and podcasters love to seek out Bea as an interviewee for her enthusiasm, personability, and articulateness. In this manner, Bea Palya, the coach and business woman, "sells" Bea Palya the popular singer, while her charisma and fame as a singer builds demand for her expertise as a coach and an entrepreneur. She makes compelling efforts to bridge the two realms, the language of musical creativity and entrepreneurism. Some critics may wonder how she can reconcile her stage personas—the "Gypsy slut" or the freedom-loving rebel—with the mindset of a straight-laced business woman? How can she be a contemporary shaman on Saturday night and morph into a speaker for Citibank employees on Monday morning? Bea admits to struggling with the often onerous task of what she calls "conscious context switches" between the creator-performer on stage or in the recording studio, and the highly structured person in the office. Added to this is a third mindset required to mother her two young children. In our interview she spoke about these shifts as "a continuous exercise in deterring catastrophes."[11] Nevertheless, Bea is confident about the credibility and compatibility of performing all these different roles. Some answers to such gendered dilemmas lie in her personal philosophy, most notably, the feminist values suffusing both her musical and extramusical work, including an emphasis on collective decision making and empathic listening at the expense of one-upmanship and self-centeredness. Skeptical about the

---

[11]Interview with Samu Gryllus and Bea Palya by authors, February 13, 2020, Budapest.

romantic masculinist myth of the artist-genius, Bea does not subscribe to the common belief that planning, scheduling, and budgeting are exclusive to musical creativity. She explains her recent accommodation of her roles by using sexual metaphors: "[My] company employs women and our most important subcontractors are the musicians; the band is all-male. Each [group] requires from me a different type of leadership ... As I've grown more whole as a person in my private life after my divorce, I've also become more feminine in business. I used to feel too masculine as the company's manager and the leader of the musical ensemble. I pushed ahead, created by way of penetration. I had this toughness in me as if I was a warrior going to battle with a sword. I still love this quality of mine but I've got softer and more attentive to the input from my environment; I have faith in the power of building connections, in the inspiring warmth of encounters, and in creativity through receiving and acceptance" (Szentgyörgyi 2019).

In this chapter we attempted to show the ongoing and increasing relevance of the gender aware voice in Bea's music and public persona, and the presumably indirect yet palpable influence of Hélèn Cixous's second-wave feminism on her songwriting—a discovery that surprised and fascinated us. Edit András (2010) has argued that, by virtue of the long isolation of Cold War Hungary from global (mostly Western) feminist thought, its influx after the regime change of 1990 triggered not only resistance but some confusion and misconceptions as to its successive waves and various branches that had never been properly sorted out for the broader public. For most Hungarian speakers, feminism is viewed as a monolithic movement and ideology. Bea, raising ideas, some of which are best and most systematically laid out in a classic text such as

Cixous's "Medusa," speaks not only to her courage and open mind as a songwriter but to her communicating challenging thoughts about female sexuality, subjecthood, and creativity. Her ideas are received as if seemingly coming from "nowhere," an impression testifying to the near-absence of public knowledge and discourse about the origins and fundamental tenets of feminism and its complicated yet thriving relationship with women-made popular music.

In 2016 Bea published a rousing article entitled "Where have the women gone"? where she bemoans the paucity of female singer-songwriters in her country, urging women musicians and singers to grab their unfinished compositions from their drawers and let their voices be heard, since those voices are crucially important. Bea has been navigating a structurally and politically difficult local popular musical terrain as one of the first female singer-songwriters with an agenda; but her work, her recognition, and increasing influence on younger women musicians is both a symptom and a promoter of ferment in the field. She has followers. Part of the reason, besides her star power, is that popular music suffers less ideological intervention by the government than symbolically more valued fields, such as literary production and theater (Barna et al. 2019). Public statements by feminist fiction writers or gay stage directors, for instance, incur harsher retaliation than those by popular songwriters.[12] A number of recent

---

[12]The critically renowned, internationally known fiction writer, Krisztina Tóth, endured vicious attacks for expressing unorthodox views about patriarchal ideals of femininity conveyed by novels in the Hungarian literary canon (Enté, 2021). The celebrated Róbert Alföldi, an openly gay director, actor, and television personality, suffered the extreme right's sustained smear campaign. He was the director of the leading National Theater of Hungary from 2008 until his politically motivated removal from his position in 2013 (Levi, 2013).

initiatives by MusicaFemina Hungary and Ladyfest Budapest, among others, frequently in collaboration with other European Union countries, also encourage women's more active and diverse participation in popular and art music. More symbolic and financial recognition is granted for female musical authors of late, detectable in the increasing number of registered female songwriters, whose percentage has tripled over four years. It is still a meager 16 percent—a figure now on a par with international trends.[13] These are tiny steps of progress yet indicate that Bea's call for change is not falling on deaf ears.

[13]See "Pop, alternatív és gyermekzene—nőiesedik a dalszerzők világa" by *Artisjus*, November 18, 2018, https://dalszerzo.hu/2015/11/18/pop-alternativ-es-gyermekzene-noiesedik-a-dalszerzok-vilaga/ (last accessed March 20, 2021).

References

Adorno, Theodor. W. 2002. "On Popular Music." *Essays on Music*. Selected with introduction, commentary, and notes by Richard Leppert. Berkeley: University of California Press.

Anderson, Benedict. 1983. *Imagined Communities. Reflections on the Origin and Spread of Nationalism*. New York: Verso.

András, Edit. 1995. "Vízpróba a kortárs (nõ)művészeten, (nõ) művészeken" In Vízpróba [Water ordeal], ed. Edit András and Gabor Andrási, A Series of Exhibitions at the Óbuda Club Gallery and at the Cellar Gallery in Óbuda. Budapest: Óbudai Társaskör 25–43.

András, Edit. 2008/2009. "An Agent that is still at Work. The Trauma of Collective Memory of the Socialist Past." In *Writing Central European Art History*. Patterns. Travelling Lecture Set. ERSTE Foundation organized by World University Service (WUS) Austria. ERSTE Stiftung Reader # 01.

András, Edit. 2010. "Gender minefield. The heritage of the past." In *Gender Check: A Reader. Art and Theory in Eastern Europe*, edited by Bojana Pejic & Erste Foundation & Museum Moderner Kunst Stiftung Ludwig Wien. Cologne: Verlag der Buchhandlung Walther König. 179–83.

Bácskai, Erika, Péter Makara, Róbert Manchin, László Váradi, and Iván Vitányi. 1969-A. *Beat*. Budapest: Zeneműkiadó.

Bácskai, Erika, Péter Makara, Róbert Manchin, László Váradi, and Iván Vitányi. 1969-B. *Az Extázis 7-től 10-ig című film fogadtatásáról*. Budapest: MRT Tömegkommunikációs Kutatóközpont.

Barna, Emilia. 2017. "A Translocal Music Room of One's Own: Female Musicians within the Budapest Lo-Fi Music Scene." In *Made in Hungary. Studies in Popular Music*, edited by Emília Barna and Tamás Tófalvy. New York: Routledge, 47–57.

Barna, Emília, Gergely Csányi, Ágnes Gagyi, and Tamás Gerőcs. 2017. "East-Central European feminist activism in the context of uneven development in the EU, and ways to move forward." In *The Future of the European Union. Feminist Perspectives from East-Central Europe*, edited by Eszter Kováts. Budapest: Friedrich-Ebert-Stiftung, 75–8.

(borzák) "Játék az ének: Palya Bea a múltba kacsintott." *Szabad Föld*, 1–2010. 439.

Boym, Svetlana. 2001. *The Future of Nostalgia*, New York: Basic Books.

Boym, Svetlana. 2007. Nostalgia and its discontents. *The Hedgehog Review*, Vol. 9, No. 2, https://hedgehogreview.com/issues/the-uses-of-the-past/articles/nostalgia-and-its-discontents (last accessed 21 Aug. 2020).

Brownstein, Carrie. 2015. *Hunger Makes Me a Modern Girl. A Memoir*. Riverhead Books, New York.

Bullock, Penn and Eli Kerry. 2017. "Trumpwave and Fashwave are Just the Latest Disturbing Examples of the Far-Right Appropriating Electronic Music." *Vice*. January 30, 2017. https://www.vice.com/amp/en_us/article/mgwk7b/trumpwave-fashwave-far-right-appropriation-vaporwave-synthwave (last accessed February 18, 2021).

Cixous, Hélène. 1976. The Laugh of the Medusa. Translated by Keith Cohen and Paula Cohen. *Signs*, Vol. 1, No. 4. (Summer), pp. 875–93. http://links.jstor.org/sici?sici=0097-9740%28197622%291%3A4%3C875%3ATLOTM%3E2.0.CO%3B2-V (last accessed March 8, 2021).

Cole, Ross. 2020. "Turning Trash into Mantras: An Interview with Vaporwave Producer Strawberry Illuminati." *ASAP/J* is the open-access platform of ASAP/Journal (Association for the Study of the Arts of the Present). January 9, 2020. Online. http://asapjournal.com/turning-trash-into-mantras-an-interview-with-vaporwave-producer-strawberry-illuminati-ross-cole (last accessed March 5, 2021).

Csóka, Ágnes, Ágnes Palotás, Ildikó Hepp, and Zsanett, Steszkó. "Zenészlányok mondják el, milyen nőként létezni a hazai zeneiparban." *Keret* July 5, 2018. http://keretblog.hu/lanyok-vs-hazai-zeneipar/keretblog.hu (last accessed February 2, 2021).

Dalos, Anna. 2015. "Nem várok holnapig!" Egy feminista olvasat-kísérlet. A "Lendület" 20–21. Századi Magyar Zenei Archívum honlapja, 1–5.

Debord, Guy. 1994. *The Society of the Spectacle*. Translation by Donald Nicholson Smith. New York, NY: Zone Books.

DeCurtis, Anthony. 1993. "Q&A: Bryan Ferry talks Eno, Dylan's modern ideas, and 'Hideous' Rap." *Rolling Stone*, July 8, 1993.

DeNora, Tia. 2000. *Music in Everyday Life*. New York: Cambridge University Press.

DeNora, Tia. 2015. *Musical Asylums. Wellbeing through Music in Everyday Life*. Ashgate, 3–4.

Dömötör, Endre. 2018. Különböző előadók: Egy dicső nemzet kifordult gyomra (lemezkritika). *Recorder*. July 18, 2018. https://recorder.blog.hu/2018/07/18/kulonbozo_eloadok_egy_dicso_nemzet_kifordult_gyomra_lemezkritika (last accessed October 31, 2020).

Elavsky, Michael C. 2011. "Musically mapped: Czech popular music as a second 'world sound.'" *European Journal of Cultural Studies* 14:3.

Enté. 2021. "Tóth Krisztina: Jókai miatt ne tegyenek kutyaszart a postaládámba!" *Index*, February 23, 2021. https://index.hu/kultur/2021/02/23/toth-krisztina-facebook-jokai-mor.

Escoffier, Jeffrey (ed). 2003. *Sexual Revolution*. Running Press.

Feischmidt, Margit and Gergő Pulay. 2017. "'Rocking the nation': the popular culture of neo-nationalism," *Nations and Nationalism*. 23 (2), 309–26.

Fisher, Mark. 2009. *Capitalist Realism: Is There No Alternative?* Zero Books, UK.

Fisher, Mark. 2013. "The Metaphysics of Crackle: Afrofuturism and Hauntology." *Dancecult: Journal of Electronic Dance Music Culture* 5 (2).

Fisher, Mark. 2014. *Ghosts of My Life. Writings on Depression, Hauntology and Lost Futures*. Zero Books. John Hunt Publishing. Kindle edition.

Fouz-Hernandez, Santiago and Freya Jarman-Ivens (ed). 2004. "Re-Invention? Madonna's drowned worlds resurface." Introduction to *Madonna's Drowned Worlds. New Approaches to her Cultural Transformations 1983–2003*. Burlington VT: Ashgate, xvii.

Gauntlett, David. 2004. "Madonna's daughters. Girl power and the empowered girl-pop breakthrough." In *Madonna's Drowned Worlds*. 168–70.

Gillett, Charlie. 1983. *The Sound of the City*. New York: Pantheon Books. 3–65.

Gorondy, Pablo. 2019. "Hungary touts family policies as alternative to immigration." *AP News*, September 5. https://apnews.com/article/279dfc17b13340e0bc272717cf75b768 (last accessed March 20, 2021).

Grow, Kory. 2018. "Angelique Kidjo Talks Reinventing Talking Heads''Remain in Light' on New LP." *Rolling Stone*, March 22,

2018. https://www.rollingstone.com/music/music-features/
angelique-kidjo-talks-reinventing-talking-heads-remain-in-
light-on-new-lp-203888 (last accessed November 4, 2020).

György, Eszter. 2020. "A magyarországi roma népzene története:
autenticitás és hibriditás." In *A magyar populáris zene
története(i). Források, módszerek, perspektívák,* edited by Ádám
Ignácz. Rózsavölgyi és Társa Kiadó, 155–88.

Hobsbawm, Eric and Terence Ranger (ed). 1983. *The Invention of
Tradition.* New York: Cambridge University Press.

Hofmeister, Zoltán. "Mi köze Osztyapenkónak a Mekihez"? *Lokál,*
2017. 07. 18. lokal.hu (last accessed June 28, 2020).

Hogarty, Jean. 2016. *Popular Music and Retro Culture in the Digital
Era.* New York: Routledge.

Horváth, Sándor. 2009. "Patchwork identities and folk devils:
youth subcultures and gangs in socialist Hungary." *Social
History,* March 2010, Vol. 34 No. 2.

Huizinga, Johan. 1949/1980. *Homo Ludens. A Study of the
Play-Element in Culture.* London, Boston, and Henley:
Routledge & Kegan Paul.

Imre, Anikó. 2002. "Hungarian poetic nationalism or national
pornography? Eastern Europe and feminism—with a
difference." In *Violence and the Body: Race, Gender, and the State,*
edited by A. J. Aldama, Indiana University Press, 39–58.

Iordanova, Dina. 2012. Preface to *A Companion to Eastern
European Cinemas,* edited by Anikó Imre, Wiley and Sons, 18.

Istvandity, Lauren. 2014. The lifetime soundtrack: Music as an
archive for autobiographical memory. *Popular Music History.*
Aug, Vol. 9 Issue 2.

James, Robin. 2020. "Music and Feminism in the 21st Century."
Music Research Annual 1: 1–25.

Jones, Steve, 2005. "Better off dead: Or, making it the hard way." In *Afterlife as Afterimage: Understanding Posthumous Fame*, edited by Steve Jones and Joli Jensen. New York: Peter Lang.

Jordan, Michael. J. 1997. "Hungary Hums Old Communist Hits. Album that fueled 'Red chic' may be released in the US." *The Christian Science Monitor*, 89, issue 21. Dec 24, 1997. https://www.csmonitor.com/1997/1224/122497.intl.intl.1.html (last accessed November, 8 2021).

Juno, Andrea. 1996. *Angry Women in Rock*. Volume One. New York: Juno Books.

Kappanyos, András. 2017. Az ellenkultúra domesztikálása. Táncdalfesztivál 1966–68. In *Populáris zene és államhatalom*, edited by Ádám Ignácz. Budapest: Rózsavölgyi, 54–72.

Karlen, Neal. 1994. *Babes in Toyland: The Making and Selling of a Rock and Roll Band*. Times Books, Random House.

Keightley, Keir. 2003. "Cover version." In *Bloomsbury Encyclopedia of Popular Music of the World*, Volume I: Media, Industry and Society, edited by John Shepherd, David Horn, Dave Laing, Paul Oliver, and Peter Wicke. New York: Continuum, Published Online: 2017. https://www.bloomsburypopularmusic.com/encyclopedia-chapter?docid=b-9781501329227&tocid=b-9781501329227-0028108&st=cover+version (last accessed Feb 21, 2021).

Koronczay, Lilla. 2014. 10+1 kérdés. *Nők Lapja*, January 29.

Kováts, Eszter. 2018. "Questioning Consensuses: Right-Wing Populism, Anti-Populism, and the Threat of 'Gender Ideology.'" *Sociological Research Online,* Rapid Response 1–11. https://doi.org/10.1177/1360780418764735 (last accessed Feb 21, 2021).

Kőbányai, János. 1979. "Biztosítótű és bőrnadrág" *Mozgó Világ* 5, no. 2: 64–77.

Kürti, László. 1991. "Rocking the State. Youth and Rock Music Culture in Hungary 1976–1990." *East-European Politics and Societies* 5, issue 3. 501–3.

Kürti, László. 2012. "Twenty years after: Rock Music and national rock in Hungary." *Region: Regional Studies of Russia, Eastern Europe, and Central Asia* 1, issue 1. 105–6.

Lange, Barbara Rose. 1996. "Lakodalmas rock and the rejection of vernacular culture in postsocialist Hungary." in *Retuning Culture. Musical Change Eastern/Central Europe*, edited by Mark Slobin. Durham: University Press, 76–91.

Lange, Barbara Rose. 2018. *Local Fusions. Folk Music Experiments in Central Europe at the Millennium*, New York: Oxford University Press.

Lange, Barbara Rose. 2020. Modes of Femininity and Power in Hungarian World Music (and U.S. Country Music). Lecture presented at the MusicaFemina International Symposium, Budapest, Hungary, January 8–9, 2020.

Lévai, Júlia and Vitányi Iván. 1972. *Miből lesz a sláger? Az elmúlt 40 év slágereinek a vizsgálata*. Budapest: Zeneműkiadó.

Levi, Jonathan. 2013. "Politics Spills Onto Stage in Budapest." *The New York Times*. April 4, 2013. https://www.nytimes.com/2013/04/05/arts/05iht-angels05.html (last accessed March 20, 2021).

Lipsitz, George. 1990. *Time Passages. Collective Memory and American Popular Culture*. Minneapolis: University of Minnesota Press.

Malawey, Victoria. 2006. "'Find out what it means to me.' Aretha Franklin's gendered re-authoring of Otis Redding's 'Respect.'" *Popular Music* (2014) vol 33/2. 2014, pp. 185–207.

Marton, László Távolodó. 2006. "Szerelem a Tiszán túl—Morotva, Söndörgő, Kiss Ferenc, Palya Bea (lemez)." in *Magyar Narancs*. June 29, 2006. https://magyarnarancs.hu/zene2/szerelem_a_tiszan_tul_-_morotva_sondorgo_kiss_ferenc_palya_bea_lemez-65716 (last accessed February 13, 2021).

Marton, László Távolodó. 2010. "Lemez—World music: úgy." In *Magyar Narancs,* May 5, 2010. https://magyarnarancs.hu/zene2/lemez_-_world_music_ugy-73809?pageId=5 (last accessed March 19, 2021).

Mendelyté, Aténé. 2019. "The Mash-up of Aesthetics, Theory and Politics in Laibach's Meta-sound." In *Mute Records: Artists, Business, History,* edited by Zuleika Beaven, Marcus O'Dair, and Richard Osborne. London: Bloomsbury Academic. 141–54.

Mihelj, Sabina. 2017. Memory, post-socialism and the media: Nostalgia and beyond. *European Journal of Cultural Studies* 2017, Vol. 20 (3) 235–51.

Mosser, Kurt. 2008. "Cover Songs: Ambiguity, Multivalence, Polysemy." *Philosophy Faculty Publications*. Paper 26. http://ecommons.udayton.edu/phl_fac_pub/26 (last accessed Oct 12, 2020).

Murányi, András and Tóth, E. Zsófia. 2018. *1968 Magyarországon. Miért hagytuk, hogy így legyen?* Scolar kiadó.

Nagy-Sándor, Zsuzsa and Pauwke Berkers. 2018. "Culture, Heritage, Art: Navigating Authenticities in Contemporary Hungarian Folk Singing." *Cultural Sociology*, Vol. 12 (3) 400–17.

Németh, Eszter. 2016. "Ez meg itten fa-re-mi." Palya Bea Psyché-lemezéről. *Jelenkor*. 59:7–8. 788–801.

O'Brien, Lucy. 1995. *She Bop. The Definitive History of Women in Rock, Pop and Soul.* New York: Penguin Group.

Padgett, Ray. 2020. Various Artists' *I'm Your Fan: The Songs of Leonard Cohen*. New York: Bloomsbury Academic.

Palya, Bea. 2011. Ribizliálom. 2nd, revised edition. Budapest: Libri Kiadó. All quotations from this book are translated by Anna Szemere.

Palya, Bea. 2016. "Hová tűntek a nők? Vendégszerzőnk: Palya Bea." Dalszerzo.hu August 19. https://dalszerzo.hu/2016/08/19/hova-tuntek-a-nok-vendegszerzonk-palya-bea/ (last accessed March 19, 2021).

Pető, Andrea. 2020. "Feminist Stories from an Illiberal State: Revoking the License to Teach Gender Studies in Hungary at a University in Exile (CEU)." In *Gender and Power in Eastern Europe. Changing Concepts of Femininity and Masculinity in Power Relations*, edited by Katharina Bluhm, Gertrud Pickhan, Justyna Stypinska, and Agnieszka Wierzcholska. Cham, Switzerland: Springer. 35–44.

Phillips, Peter. 2006. "Importance of hummability." *The Spectator*, January 7. https://www.spectator.co.uk/article/importance-of-hummability (last accessed February 23, 2021).

Plasketes, George. 2005. "Re-flections on the Cover Age: A Collage of Continuous Coverage in Popular Music." *Popular Music and Society*, vol. 28:2, 137–61.

Podhorányi, Zsolt. 2010. "Mintha tóban mártóztunk volna meg. A hetvenes évek világára emlékezik új, Én leszek a játékszered című lemezén Palya Bea." *Népszava*, March 11.

Polgár, Tibor. 1980. "Miből lesz a sláger." *Chicago és Környéke*, 07. 26., issue 30, 11.

Raine, Sarah and Catherine Strong (ed). 2018. "Gender Politics in the Music Industry." Special issue. *IASPM Journal* 8, No 1.

Ramet, Sabrina. 2005. *Thinking about Yugoslavia: Scholarly Debates about the Yugoslav Breakup and the Wars in Bosnia and Kosovo*. New York: Cambridge University Press.

Reynolds, Simon. 2011. *Retromania. Pop Culture's Addiction to Its Own Past*. New York: Farrar, Straus and Giroux. Kindle edition.

Rogers, Mary F. 1999. *Barbie Culture*. Thousand Oaks, CA: Sage Publications.

Rónai András. 2010. "Gizikék nélkül nem ugyanaz.": Interjú Palya Beával és Gryllus Samuval. *Quart*, March 20. https://quartarchiv.com/2021/08/13/gizikek-nelkul-nem-ugyanaz-palya-bea-es-gryllus-samu-a-quartnak/.

Rónai, András. 2014. "Palya Bea egybetereli a nőket." *Origo*, January 6, 2014. https://www.origo.hu/kultura/20140106-palya-bea-hivlak-teged-videoklip.html.

Rónai, András. 2017. "The Insecure Village Girl who Found Success and her Gentle Deconstructions." In *Made in Hungary*. 99–110.

Sipos, Balázs. 2010. "A Happy Birthday-csárdás." *168 óra*, 2. 186.

Smith-Prei, Carrie and Maria Stehle. 2016. *Awkward Politics. Technologies of Popfeminist Activism*. Montreal: McGill-Queen's University Press.

Spaskovska, Ljubica. 2011. Stairway to Hell: The Yugoslav Rock Scene and Youth during the Crisis Decade of 1981–1991. *East Central Europe* 38, 355–72.

Stanyek, Jason and Benjamin Piekut 2010. "Deadness: Technologies of the Intermundane." *TDR: The Drama Review*, Spring, Volume 54:1, 14–38.

Szemere, Anna. 2000. "'It's Yesterday's Train That's Late': Underground Rock and the Changing Face of Art Theory in Hungary." In *ArtMargins*. June 4, 2020.

Szemere, Anna. 2010. The Velvet Prison in Hindsight: Artistic Discourse in Hungary in the 1990s. In *Postsocialist Nostalgia*. edited by Maria Todorova and Zsuzsa. Gille. New York: Berghahn Books. 244–63.

Szemere, Anna. 2018. "Let's turn Hegel from His Head onto His Feet: Hopes, Myths, and Memories of the 1960s in Tamás Cseh's Musical Album 'A Letter to My Sister'." *Slavic Review,* vol. 77.

Szemere, Anna. 2020. "'But he has nothing on at all!' Underground videos targeting Viktor Orbán, Hungary's celebrity politician." *Celebrity Studies*. 11:3. 5.

Szemere, Anna and Kata Márta Nagy. 2017. "Setting Up a Tent in the 'New Europe': The Sziget Festival of Budapest." In *Made in Hungary*. 15–26.

Szentgyörgyi, Rita. 2019. "Palya Bea: Másokra mutogatás helyett, fordítsuk az ujjunkat magunk felé." *Boom Magazine*. June 24, 2019. https://boomonline.hu/content/palya-bea-masokra-mutogatas-helyett-forditsuk-az-ujjunkat-magunk-fele (last accessed February 2, 2021).

Szily, Nóra. 2021. "Palya Bea: Drága férfiak, adjátok meg nekünk a szent elszállás lehetőségét." *Femina*, March 4, 2021. https://femina.hu/kapcsolat/palya-bea-interju/ (last accessed March 16, 2021). Trans. by A.S.

Szőnyei, Tamás 2006. "Táncdalfesztivál: Már fájl minden csók." *Filmvilág*. August 22–24.

Todorova, Maria. 2010. "Introduction: From Utopia to Propaganda and Back." In *Post-Communist Nostalgia*. 1–14.

Tóth, Eszter Zsófia. 2010. *Kádár leányai. Nők a szocialista időszakban*. Budapest: Nyitott Könyvműhely, 13–33.

Vance, Carole, S. (ed) 1984. *Pleasure and Danger. Exploring Female Sexuality*. Boston: Routledge and Kegan Paul.

Verdery, Katherine. 1999. *The Political Lives of Dead Bodies. Reburial and Postsocialist Change*. New York: Columbia University Press.

Völgyi, Vera. 2014."Sejtjeinkben van a szeretés." Palya Beával Völgyi Vera beszélget. *Nők Lapja Évszakok*. Spring 16:1. 14–17.

Walker, Shaun. 2020. "Hungarian government mounts new assault on LGBT rights." *The Guardian*, November 11, 2020. https://www.theguardian.com/world/2020/nov/11/ hungarian-government-mounts-new-assault-on-lgbt-rights (last accessed March 20, 2021).

Whiteley, Sheila. 2005. *Too Much Too Young. Popular Music, Age and Gender*. New York: Routledge.

Wolff, Larry. 1994. *Inventing Eastern Europe: The Map of Civilization on the Mind of the Enlightenment*. Stanford, CA: Stanford University Press.

Yaqin, Amina. 2007. "Islamic Barbie: The Politics of Gender and Performativity." *Fashion Theory*, 11, Issue 2/3. 173–88.

Zeisler, Andi. 2008. *Feminism and Pop Culture*. Berkeley, CA: Seal Press.

Track listing of "I'll Be Your Plaything"

18 Mama (Mom) (2:11).

19 Undorító hangom van nekem (I Have a Disgusting Voice) (0:21).

20 Part-Time Lover (4:29).

21 Nem ismeri? (Don't You Know?) (0:07).

22 Nagy utazás (The Great Journey) (6:05).

23 For Philip S. (0:31).

24 Amerika (4:26).

25 Finding a Path (3:27).

26 Amerika (1:02).

27 Szőke Anni balladája (The Ballad of Blond Annie) (5:04).

28 Add már, Uram, az esőt! (Oh Lord, Give Us Some Rain!) (4:20).

29 Az eső és én (The Rain and Me) (5:12).

30 Az élet megy tovább (instrumentális) (Life Goes On— instrumental) (1:14).

31 A szerelmeseknek a legszebb dala (The Most Beautiful Song for Lovers) (0:09).

32 Megáll az idő (Time Stands Still) (5:03).

Available on CD and on all major streaming platforms, with the exception of "The Ballad of Blond Annie," which is available on the compilation Amikor én még kissrác voltam [When I was a little kid] (3T 983 142 9, 2005).

Discography

Bea Palya Solo Discography

Palya Beáta. Ágról-ágra. Tradition in motion. Orpheia ORP003BEA1, 2003.

Palya Bea. Álom-álom, kitalálom (énekelt mese). Gryllus Publishing GCD 038, 2004.

Palya Bea, Weöres Sándor. Psyché. Gryllus GCD 050/Hangzó Helikon HE 1046, 2005 (book with CD).

Palya Bea. Szeretetből jöttél erre a világra. Gryllus , GCD 069, 2007.

Palya Bea. Adieu les complexes. Sony Music 88697547532/Naïve WN145120, 2008.

Palya Bea. Egyszálének/Justonevoice. Sony Music 88697536052, 2009.

Palya Bea. Én leszek a játékszered. Sony Music 88697642232, 2010.

Palya Bea. Ezeregy szefárd éjszaka. Sony Music 88725450492, 2012.

Palya Bea. Ribizliálom (compilation), Sony Music 88697974532, 2011.

Palya Bea. Altatok—Dalok, versek Álomország kapuján innen és túl. Kolibri Gyerekkönyvkiadó, 2012 (book with CD).

Palya Bea. Nő. Palya Bea Production PBPE001, 2014.

Palya Bea. Tovább Nő. Palya Bea Production PBPE003, 2016.

Palya Bea. Nappali dalok. Bookline, 2016 (book with CD).

Palya Bea. Hazatalálok. Palya Bea Production PBPE004, 2018.

Palya Bea. Élet. Palya Bea Production PBPE008, 2020.

Other discs mentioned

Various Artists. Best of Communism. Válogatott mozgalmi dalok/A Selection of Revolutionary Songs. Gong HCD 37898, 1997.

Various Artists. Best of Communism vol. 2. Hungaroton HCD 37921, 1998.

Index